D1434226

WHO'S FEEDING WHOM?

Other titles in the **Inside Out Meditation** series:

Who's Feeding Whom?

Meic Pearse

solway

British Library Cataloguing in Publication Data

A catalogue record for this book is available from the British Library.

ISBN 1-900507-20-X

Typeset by Photoprint, Torquay, Devon
and Printed in the UK by Guernsey Press Ltd.

Preface

To anyone who has written a book like this one, the sight of one's own name out there in splendid isolation on the title cover looks faintly absurd. *Who's Feeding Whom?* owes so much to so many people that listing them all would be hard, but what follows will have to do.

Peter Amoss read through many of these ideas before this book was even a twinkle in its author's eye. He thought he was helping me to put together a reasonable sermon and, at the time, he was. But one thing leads to another. . . .

My wife Ann went well beyond the call of wifely duty in making space for me to ensure this was finished. She, Dr. Peter Cotterell, Sue Palmer and Mary Shepherd read much or all of the manuscript, and made a large number of helpful suggestions, thereby rescuing me from many errors. My friend and colleague Dr. Conrad Gempf was the source of many of the ideas on John.21.1–10 which are presented in the chapter 'Bring the Fish You Have Caught'.

All of the churches and Christian groups that have allowed me to share in their life over the years have contributed in countless ways that they can hardly know of. Being part of Linden Christian Fellowship in Swansea for more than half of my Christian life has shaped my outlook and thinking on most of the issues discussed here, though I doubt whether even they would want to be responsible for every syllable that follows.

Finally, I owe a huge debt of gratitude to those whom I laughingly call 'my students', many of whom in fact teach me more than I could ever teach them, and several of whom have discussed with me in depth many of the issues raised here. To four of them in particular, this book is dedicated with love and gratitude.

Contents

To Mary Shepherd, Colin Veysey
Kate Dunwoody and Sue Palmer –
my students, my teachers,
. . . my friends

And it would be enough for me
Thus long to live, and then to meet;
My strongest faith can scarce believe
That future days might be as sweet
As those you've lately sent.

And long it was my prayer, my mark,
To be your tool, to ride your wind.
And now with public men I walk,
And brothers ask to know my mind;
Is this your answer, Lord?

For pride, and fear of pride, do gnaw
My conscience, put me to a stand.
And whose the glory? Is it sure
Insatiate self will not demand
Some secret, subtle share?

If grasps this clay the potter's crown,
It were enough, Lord; take me now.

Meic Pearse, March 1995

Introduction

The word 'ministry' is bandied about in Christian circles to an almost sickening degree. It is an 'in' word amongst house-church (or new-church) people who wish (rightly, as I think) to emphasize the corporate nature of the body of Christ; so we have 'body ministry'. The word is in vogue amongst those charismatics who wish to point to the healing and converting power of the Holy Spirit; and so we have 'power ministry'. At the end of meetings, many Christians feel it important to pray for one another (obviously a good thing) with the expectation, especially since the advent of the 'Toronto blessing', of dramatic results; we make space for 'a time of ministry'. Our star performers on the preaching and worship-leading circuit have 'an anointed ministry', whilst the rest of us lesser lights work hard at defining, refining (and often surreptitiously magnifying) our own 'ministry'. Regular monthly and quarterly journals are dedicated to encouraging 'excellence in ministry' as if, like banking or dentistry, it were some kind of a profession. And of course in the evangelical marketplace, it is.

Ministry has become far too self-conscious. That may seem an odd remark to make at the beginning of a book which is all about focusing on ministry. But I mean the words quite literally. Most of our thinking about ministry focuses on the one doing the ministering. It is quite literally *self*-conscious. As long as I am seeking *my* ministry, hoping to refine it so that *it* becomes better and more admirable, asking God's blessing upon *it* (and so really upon me!), then I have not begun to take hold of Jesus' call upon my life at all. 'Ministry' means 'service'; most of us know this, especially when we recall the AV translation of Matthew 20.28: 'The Son of man came not to be ministered unto, but to minister, and to give his life a ransom for many.' Modern translations use the word 'serve' instead of 'minister', and ministry is about serving. If we were to be asked whether we would rather minister than be 'ministered unto', many of us would say 'yes'; if the choice were between serving and being served, we would be a lot less sure. If the words mean the same, why the difference? It is because 'ministry' has come to mean, in our modern evangelical vocabulary, almost anything but serving.

What is certain is that we cannot really serve as long as we are thinking about ourselves. In the modern West, however, we inhabit a culture of narcissism in which everything—education, TV, magazines, advertisements —teaches us to improve our social status and the feelings that we have about ourselves and that others have about us. Our activities are simply means and techniques (and oh, how we love techniques!) to that end. Modern (or rather, postmodern) thinking has 'deconstructed' our attitudes towards even our best activities, so that all work for charitable organizations, for instance, now stands unmasked as attempts by the 'helpers' to assuage their guilt feelings about the deprivation of others, or to find some sense of fulfilment, or achievement, or to create feelings of obligation in others, or to affirm their own moral superiority. Anything, in fact, except actually helping someone else. Of course, our good deeds *may* conceal any or all of these impulses, but as Christians we could never concede that all social relations are simply masks for the 'will to power'.

Nevertheless, this way of thinking has caused us all to focus upon ourselves, and not the job in hand. As a result, we have ministry-superstars. Attention and limelight are focused upon *them*, rather than upon the service they are allegedly performing or—what is even more to the point—upon Jesus, whose badge they own. And the rest of us follow them. We too want 'excellence in ministry'. We too want to do a 'professional' job by employing the right techniques. We too want public recognition, whilst acknowledging, *of course*, that it's all the Lord's handiwork in us! As I said, ministry is highly self-conscious.

But Jesus calls us to feed his lambs, not our own egos. Too often I have heard my fellow-Christians agonizing over finding their roles; we want to 'feel we're doing something', as opposed to wanting to *do something*. The difference is more than semantic; the latter attitude is conscious, the former only self-conscious. It is tempting to suggest that self-consciousness is altogether the opposite of real consciousness; that absorption in ourselves excludes real awareness of others, to whom Jesus is calling us to minister. Certainly the self-conscious attitude is a reflection of the obsessive self-absorption of our times. Experts on the New Age think that many of its religious practices are a form of self-worship, but one does not need to be an adherent of New Age thinking to be affected by the Western mind-set that has made its rise possible. And so we late twentieth-century Western Christians think that salvation, the church, and even ministry—which is, after all, serving *Jesus*—are, somehow, all about *me*. Not a few of us need to ask, in the course of our ministries, big or small, exalted or unnoticed, 'Who's this really all for?' Jesus did not say 'Look at all these idle workers; let me find some white fields for them to help them find fulfilment.' His emphasis was on the fields, and on the work that needed doing. Who will forget themselves and their own agendas, and go to work in them?

Not too long ago, I started teaching full-time at an evangelical theological college. I had been studying my area of specialization long and hard, and had done my postgraduate studies and research. I saw myself as an academic—God's academic, an academic with a message, to be sure, but still primarily as a scholar who would help evangelicals to think through the implications of their faith in my particular area of study. And I still think that.

But something has happened. My starting point had been ideas. I am set alight by ideas, insights I have gained by a combination of prayer and study and reading and discussion and debate. My danger was—and still is—of seeing the students who have come to the college where I teach, to prepare and be equipped for ministries of their own, as so much cannon fodder, ready to be bombarded with the things that I have discovered to be important. But I have needed to learn that what really confronts me is people. None of them is a blank sheet for me to write upon. Each person has a history and experiences of their own. Each is a unique child of God. Their needs go well beyond what I perceive as the scope of 'my ministry': encouragement and confidence-building for the bruised reeds, faith-building for the confused, hospitality and a listening ear for those with problems, discipline for the lazy or overbearing, plenty of love for all of them. Their very capacities to learn the things that I am so eager to teach them in class vary, according to differences in intelligence, temperament and background. As long as I am thinking only about my academic discipline and the exciting things they can learn from it, I am treating these brothers and sisters as objects, as a means to an end (and my end at that, rather than God's, if I'm not careful).

I cannot write my glorious academic career on the blank paper of their lives. And yet that is precisely what far too many of us—whatever our ministry—are attempting to do to those we claim to serve. Instead I am called, as you are, to feed Jesus' lambs. Not force-feeding; just feeding. The shepherd cannot 'wow' a group of lambs and leave them in stunned adulation. Each lamb needs to be handled individually. And their needs are wider than my gifting. As long as I am ministering from my strength alone, there is the danger that it is I who am in charge. Certainly 'I' will be the focus. But having to care for people on the basis of their need rather than my self-proclaimed and circumscribed 'ministry' forces me back onto the resources of Jesus. And can we think that that is not where Jesus intended us to be all along?

PART I

Feed My Lambs:
the Call of Jesus

ONE

Bring the Fish You Have Caught

Early in the morning, Jesus stood on the shore, but the disciples did not realize that it was Jesus.
He called out to them, 'Friends, haven't you any fish?'
'No,' they answered.
He said, 'Throw your net on the right side of the boat and you will find some.' When they did, they were unable to haul the net in because of the large number of fish.
Then the disciple whom Jesus loved said to Peter, 'It is the Lord!' ...
When they landed, they saw a fire of burning coals there with fish on it, and some bread.
Jesus said to them, 'Bring some of the fish you have just caught.' (Jn.21.4–7, 9–10)

God often seems to go to a huge amount of trouble to do things that don't seem to us to have much real purpose. He sends an angel to speak to Cornelius the centurion in Cæsarea and then, having got the soldier exactly where he wants him, trembling in fear, asking 'What is it, Lord?' and ready to do whatever he's told, he doesn't just 'give him the gospel', and get him to sign up to follow Jesus there and then. Goodness knows (or more precisely, *God* knows) he could have done! Instead, the angel tells Cornelius to send for Peter in Joppa, so that Peter can do the explaining instead. What a round-about way of doing things! It might have been easier to understand if Peter had been willing to go but, as we know, he wasn't, and God had to give Peter a special vision to explain the deal before he could get him even to associate with a Gentile. Speaking personally, if I'd been God—and I know it's just as well things are the way they are—I wouldn't have organized it like that!

Knowing that God doesn't share my insistence on efficiency, I was none too surprised when a friend of mine pointed out something in the first thirteen verses of John 21 that I hadn't noticed before. The episode describes events after Jesus' initial appearances to his disciples following his resurrection. The chapter opens with Simon Peter and six others going out for a spot of night-fishing on the Sea of Tiberias. The catch was pretty minimal: zero, in fact. As day breaks, the disciples see a man on the shore who calls out to them, asking if they have any fish, and in one short syllable they apprise him of the situation. Jesus (for it is, of course, he) must have been cheating and using his omniscience; at any rate, the way he phrases the question—'Haven't you any fish?'— seems to indicate he knew, and was just checking. (Maybe the way the boat was lying high in the water showed they hadn't landed too many whales.) He then organizes a miraculous catch by telling them to throw their nets over the other side of the boat, and they recognize who he is. Then comes the crazy, inefficient part that, even more than the miracle, seems to be a sure mark of divine activity. He tells the disciples (vv.9–10) to bring some of the fish they have caught to the break-fast, even though he already has some cooking on a fire before they get there! What's the point? Miracles for the fun of it? What games is he playing with these men who have been his closest companions for three years?

The point of it all is this: Jesus can do anything, *any*thing at all, including providing those fish in any one of a hundred different ways, but he wants to include and involve his friends.

And we are his friends. There'll be breakfast whether you help or not, but Jesus wants some of the fish *you* have caught. The angel could have converted Cornelius; given that Peter was as awkward and hidebound as he was, it would probably have been easier without him anyway. But God wanted to act through Peter. Similarly, he chooses to act through us, and is unwilling to act without us. What he wants is our co-operation. He doesn't, in a philosophical sense, *need* our co-operation, any more than he needs food or sleep. But, by becoming man, he chose to need food and sleep, and is recorded as becoming hungry and tired when he didn't get them. In the same way, he has chosen to need us, not because he's not omnipotent, but because God isn't the sort of efficiency-juggernaut that I'm sometimes crazy enough to think I'd prefer (prefer, that is, as long as I'm contemplating his dealings with other people, and not with me). He loves us, and chooses to involve us in his activities. What fish will you bring to the breakfast?

What do *you* have that you can contribute to what Jesus is doing? This is the only real basis for ministry. What Jesus is doing right now may seem as trivial to you as cooking breakfast. But 'ministry' is not about your self-aggrandizement; the focus is upon what Jesus is doing, not upon you. There are already fish on the fire. Will you become part of what Jesus is doing? Will you bring what you have to serve Jesus through serving others?

As Christians, we are familiar with the wonderful truth that Jesus has come to reconcile us to God by taking the punishment for our sins upon himself. But the apostle Paul explicitly told the Corinthian Christians that God has committed to *us* 'the ministry of reconciliation' (2 Cor.5.18–19). The point is that, though this is divine work, God chooses to do it through his people—

and that means you and me. Paul's fellow apostle, Peter, made the same basic point: he said that 'each one should use whatever gift he has received to serve others', and that when we do so we are 'faithfully administering God's grace' (1 Pet.4.10). Part of my ministry is to write this book, and it is my prayer that, as you read it, God's grace will be administered to your heart and life. Perhaps such an idea is not too strange to us, for we often use this kind of language in respect of sermons, and a book such as this is only a printed sermon. (Indeed, it is; I have preached on this subject many times!) 'But', many will say, 'my ministry is not so public. How can it be administering God's grace?' Peter assures us that it does. If we do something that few people see, we tend to diminish its value, forgetting to view what is happening through the eyes of Jesus, whose opinion is the only one that counts. So if I put up the acetates on the overhead projector, or spend time praying for others, or do the gardening for an old person, or give hospitality to visitors, or arrange the seats for the meetings, I do not see my actions in an eternal perspective. And, as others look at me doing these things, neither do they. But we are all wrong. As each one of us uses our gifts in the service of others, we are 'faithfully administering God's grace'.

Let none of us be tempted to think that such thoughts are a mere consolation for those whose service in the church is inconspicuous. For they come as part of a command. Jesus told the parable of the master going on a journey, and giving different talents to his servants (Matt.25.14–15). On his return, he wanted to know what had been done with them, and there were serious consequences for those who had neglected to use what had been entrusted to them. The point is clear: Jesus wants to use us in bringing 'the ministry of reconciliation', building up the church, bringing love and healing to the broken, 'administering God's grace'. Jesus is cooking breakfast. Will you bring the fish that you have caught to be a part of it?

* * *

There is another thing we should notice about that strange breakfast by the lakeside. As Simon Peter brought his fish ashore, he couldn't help but be aware that they were fresh and straight from the water. He had a hundred and fifty-three big ones (Jn.21.11). Jesus doesn't appear to have had a boat, so *his* fish must have been caught some hours before, at least. Jesus had just a few, partly cooked, older ones. So Simon Peter can't have helped thinking (or rather, knowing) that his own fish would taste better than those which Jesus had—*so* well-meaningly—provided.

Let nobody be shocked at such an impious thought. We do the same thing all the time. 'It's great that you're here, Lord, but actually I can do this better myself.' We have our lives all planned out, possibly in a way that we are sure is 'serving the Lord'. Then he comes and tells us to do something else, but we are unwilling to hear him because we are taken up with our own schemes. It was David Watson who said that, if the Holy Spirit were taken out of the church, ninety per cent of our activities would carry on just as before. If God moves upon one of our services, the instinct is to keep to our schedule anyway: there is a sermon that has been prepared, so it had better be given, there is a list of pre-prepared choruses which the worship leaders are impatient to be working through, and there are dinners waiting at home. 'It's great that you're here, Lord, but we've got a schedule to keep to.' We're all familiar with over-reliance on human giftings in the church. Worship-leading gets unthinkingly assigned to technically and musically competent pianists, who may have little or no spiritual 'feel' for the direction in which the worship is going. The pulpit gets monopolized by a man (and it usually *is* a man) with a training in homiletics. In the same way, relatively little emphasis is given to the importance of befriending and loving relationships in healing deep hurts; churches are much more anxious to develop formalized counselling systems with external accreditation. Now I don't wish to minimize the importance of any of these technical skills (if I did then the last place I'd choose to work would be a theological college!), but I'm pointing out that we often make the mistake of relying on them more than on Jesus.

If Simon Peter made the same mistake with his fish, then he would have been forgetting something: *all* of the fish had been provided by Jesus! The hundred and fifty-three were a miraculous catch that Jesus had just engineered. In the same way, the very gifts that you and I have, the very things that we bring to him for the service of his kingdom, are themselves gifts from a loving God. Do you preach? Then your mind, your rhetorical and didactic skills, not to mention the spiritual anointing upon your ministry, are all gifts from the very Jesus that you are called to preach, and whose people you are called to feed. Do you disciple new Christians? Then your interpersonal skills, your ability to inspire confidence in others—often an ability to relate to a particular type of person that others cannot, your grasp of the basics of the faith and ability to impart spiritual disciplines: these are all gifts from the very Jesus to whom you point others. Do you have a ministry of intercession? Then it is God who has worked together the various strands of your life to produce this good: your ability to persevere in prayer, the love that drives you on, your knowledge of the Scriptures, perhaps even some of the circumstances which you may perceive as disadvantages—time and relative immobility—to propel you in the direction of this work. Do you give hospitality? Then your home, its welcoming atmosphere, your gifts in preparing food, in encouraging others and all of the other elements that go to make up this ministry have all been given to you by the One who promised that even a cup of water given in his name will not go unrewarded. Whatever your area of service—and clearly, the list could be extended indefinitely—your best efforts, which Jesus wants and often seems to refuse to act without, are also a provision of God, because he gave you the talents, abilities, gifts and ministries in the first place. Bring your fish to the breakfast, but remember who provided them!

TWO

A Question of Love

When they had finished eating, Jesus said to Simon Peter, 'Simon son of John, do you truly love me more than these?' 'Yes, Lord,' he said, 'you know that I love you.' Jesus said, 'Feed my lambs.'
Again Jesus said, 'Simon son of John, do you truly love me?'
He answered, 'Yes, Lord, you know that I love you.'
Jesus said, 'Take care of my sheep.'
The third time he said to him, 'Simon son of John, do you love me?'
Peter was hurt because Jesus asked him the third time, 'Do you love me?' He said, 'Lord, you know all things; you know that I love you' (Jn.21.15–17).

The Unavoidable Question

After the breakfast, Jesus takes Peter on one side and asks him the famous repeated question, 'Do you love me?' No more important question can be asked of anyone, and it's one that comes to all of us sooner or later. There is no limit to the ways in which God wants to use us, whoever and wherever we are. Within the church is a whole kaleidoscope of different kinds of

16

ministries: some public, some unseen; some using or requiring large amounts of training or preparation, some not; and every possible combination of natural and supernatural giftings, enhanced by practice and prayer. It's exciting. But all of this is hopeless and pointless if it doesn't flow out of a deeper love for Jesus. And this is why Jesus asks the question that he does. Jesus wants to exhort Peter to 'Feed my lambs', but the very giving of the instruction itself is dependent upon a positive answer to the question 'Do you love me?' So first comes the question, and after Peter's repeated answer 'Yes', Jesus tells him on each occasion to feed the flock. The point is this: your ministry and mine have to be rooted first and foremost in a love for Jesus, or they are no ministries at all. Jesus is saying, 'I must be the focus of your attention, not your "ministry". Your ministry may—or may not—provide you with fulfilment, but that is not the point. If you focus upon "being fulfilled", then you are still preoccupied with yourself. But I have come to call you out of preoccupation with the self. I want you to ground yourself in me, and through that to learn to give yourself away for others.' Only if we are in love with Jesus will we get hold of his heart for people, and only then will we be able to feed his lambs.

The first time Jesus puts the question to Peter, he asks 'Do you love me more than these?' and scholars debate what Jesus meant by 'these'. 'Do you love me more than the others do?' Or alternatively, 'Do you, Peter, love me more than you love the others?' There is a third possibility: 'Do you love me more than you love this fishing equipment?' Probably the first is correct; before the crucifixion, Peter had been anxious to prove that he was more devoted to Jesus than the others were. He had protested (Matt.26.33) that, 'even if all fall away on account of you, I never will.' But by the fire in the high-priest's courtyard, that had proved to be a very empty boast. Peter, too, had feet of clay.

The point of Jesus' repeated question is that it opened up Peter's heart. It opens up ours as well. For a start, it reminded Peter of the weakness of his own love. Are we, like Peter, tempted to see ourselves in the heroic mould? 'The others around us may be a sham, Jesus. I can see their failings so clearly. But—and I know I've got my faults as well—at least I'll stick with it come what may.' Is that how we think? Well, forget it. I'm completely unreliable, and so are you. And so was Peter. Of course Jesus wants Peter's love—that's why he keeps asking the question. But our love is too weak to become an object of faith in itself. No, only Jesus is fit to be the repository of our confidence. To rely upon 'our love for Jesus', rather than upon Jesus himself, is to fall prey to the introspective, self-aware tendency once more.

In the second place, the questioning forced Peter to consider, and to realize that, despite his own extreme fallibility, he really did love Jesus. Part of the reason my friends love me is because I love them. Conversely, part of the reason I love them is because they love me. But my relationship with Jesus doesn't work on quite the same basis. Jesus has loved me all along, regardless of whether I have loved him or not. Not only was my life as a non-Christian spent ignoring Jesus, but I wince to think how much of it still falls far short of really putting him first. So if I *am* to give him my love, then it is not to earn his love in return, for I have it already. In any case, to do it in order to get something else in return would be a fool's errand, for my love is so unreliable I would stand little chance of getting what I wanted through it. In any case, would loving Jesus (or anyone else) really be love at all if it were done with an eye to getting something out of it?

'And yet,' someone will protest, 'you have just told us that we *must* love Jesus if we are to be of any use in "feeding his lambs". Isn't that done with an eye to getting something out of it?' Certainly it could be. Certainly, too, Jesus wants us to love him for himself, not as a means to something else, such as 'ministry'. But that paradox is taken up in the third thing that Jesus' repeated question does to Peter: it forces him to cast

himself upon Jesus' all-knowingness. In response to
being asked for the third time 'Do you love me?', Peter
responds by saying, in effect, 'I think I love you, Lord—
you alone know', just as someone else had once said to
Jesus, 'Lord, I do believe, help me overcome my un-
belief' (Mk.9.24).

Our very best actions are mixed-motive affairs. With
what motives will we undertake to 'feed Jesus' lambs'? I
often ask myself: what are my motives for preaching
and teaching others? Love for Jesus? Concern for others?
Is it 'concern for truth'? How about eagerness to put
across *my perception* of the truth? (Notice how we're
getting just a shade less worthy all the time?) What
about self-aggrandizement and a desire to be thought
well of? Or are our motives a mixture of all of these
things? What can we say for ourselves? Like Peter I need
to say, 'Lord, you know all things. You alone see it—
even after I've searched and searched my own heart,
after I've sought to eradicate all evil motives and to act
only from what is good—you alone see the true state of
my heart.' Depressed? We shouldn't be, because there is
good news. I don't know whether John was listening in
on the conversation between Peter and Jesus. Personally,
I doubt it. But what is certain is that he was close by, for
Peter was to point him out a few moments later. And
John it was who later wrote on the basis of his own
experience that, even if 'our hearts condemn us, he is
greater than our hearts' (1 Jn.3.20). Every time I read or
think of that verse, my heart gives a leap, for it means
that I, even I, am OK after all! Jesus sees all the nasty
ambiguities in my heart and my motivations, and even
the really dark places about which there is no ambiguity
at all. And he is not shocked. As Gerald Coates loves to
put it, 'He is never disillusioned about us, because he
was never under any illusions in the first place.' My
friends know that, if ever I fall under the proverbial bus,
1 John 3.20 goes on the tombstone!

And so Peter says, 'Lord, you know all things; you
know that I love you.' You can almost hear him add

desperately under his breath, 'I think!' 'Good', says Jesus. 'Here's what I want you to do for me. Feed my sheep. I'm going to fill you with my love for others.'

Loving Others

Easy, isn't it? Well, sometimes, it really is. Lovely people are easy to love, and I know plenty of them. With some of them, it would be much harder *not* to love them than the reverse. Many people who know my wife and me think that we have a great ministry of hospitality, because quite a number of those with whom we come into contact find their way back to our house for a meal, or to spend the day with us. But things are not so simple, for there is a mixture of motives here as with so much else that we all do. An element of the 'hospitality' is pure selfishness. Eight or nine times out of ten, people get asked around because we like them. My wife and I get to meet a lot of young committed Christians, and if we think 'Wow! This is a real quality person; let's get to know them better', then we ask them over. Hebrews 13.2 talks about entertaining angels in disguise, but if the disguise is a little too thick, frankly, we leave them where they are for someone else to look after. A few exceptions apart, only where the disguise is barely paper-thin do we begin to take an interest.

Now, you don't need to be a perceptive genius to realize that there is no particular spiritual merit in all of this. It's not a text often preached on, but Jesus has some advice for those of us with ministries of hospitality: 'When you give a luncheon or dinner, do not invite your friends, your brothers or relatives, or your rich neighbours; if you do, they may invite you back and so you will be repaid. But when you give a banquet, invite the poor, the crippled, the lame, the blind, and you will be blessed. Although they cannot repay you, you will be repaid at the resurrection of the righteous' (Lk.14.12–14). To love the lovely, or to befriend the friendly, is not spiritual (or unspiritual); it's simply a natural response. 'If you love those who love you,' says Jesus, 'what reward will you get? Are not even the tax collectors doing that? And if you greet only your brothers, what are you doing more than others? Do not even pagans do that?' (Matt.5.46–47). There's nothing wrong, of course, with befriending the appealing, the intelligent, the gifted and the attractive. As a matter of fact it's a good thing. Just don't expect rewards in heaven for it, because it is its own reward right now.

But how about the unlovely? Who wants to care for them? Minister to them? Befriend them? It sounds a great idea in the abstract, but who wants to do it in the concrete? Sometime ago I was faced with two pastoral crises in the same week. The first involved two individuals about whom I care very much. Both of them are wonderful people, but they were getting into a tangle with one another, and one of them called me in to help. What I could do didn't amount to very much in practice, largely because my actions were overtaken by events, but I was certainly willing to do all that was possible. My attitude towards the problem was 'A1', and this fact was appreciated by those involved. Why? Because I love them. Later that week, I was confronted with another call for help, but this time everything was different . . . at least from my point of view. In this case, the people involved were a little odd, they had all kinds of problems which I did not (and do not) have the faith to see resolved, and I find the woman, in particular, very irritating in her manner, even though I know she can't help it. As she explained her side of the story, I felt as if I were part of a cartoon strip, with thought balloons emerging from my head; the thoughts in them were not polite! Out of duty, I made some gesture in the direction of 'help', so I could certainly defend myself by saying I had done something. But I knew, and they suspected, that I really did not want to be bothered. Why the big difference in attitude? Because these were the unlovely, and my love was found wanting.

There are, of course, no easy and glib answers as to what to do when everything inside us says, 'I don't want very much to do with this person.' Nevertheless, Jesus insists that, if we love him, we will feed his sheep. Jesus' own example may help us here: he didn't wait for us to become lovable before moving out towards us in love. If he had, well . . . not to put too fine a point upon it, he'd be waiting still! The apostle Paul pointed out to the Roman Christians that, 'While we were still sinners, Christ came and died for us. . . . When we were God's enemies, we were reconciled to him through the death of his Son' (Rom.5.8, 10). It's just as well Jesus didn't cast around to see who was agreeable company before deciding whom he would bless with his presence, and whom he would minister to. We may call ourselves God's people but, as we look into our own hearts, it's pretty obvious that he doesn't exactly keep the best of company even now! And we'd better be grateful for that fact.

The actions of Jesus do more than merely make us feel depressed because of our own natural inability to follow his example. Because of what Jesus has done, Paul says, 'God has poured out his love into our hearts by the Holy Spirit' (Rom.5.5). The plan is that we are now free to go and do the same, because the kind of love that took Jesus to the cross for repulsive people like you and me is now present in the hearts of its beneficiaries: you and me! If we are willing to allow his love to live in us— allow ourselves to be transformed by a love relationship with Jesus—then we can, and will, feed his sheep, whether they're ugly customers or not. After twenty years as a Christian, I'm still dumb enough to think that's good news.

The triumph of the nagging doubts

It's a pretty big deal to ask someone the same question three times in the space of a few minutes. But then, there

are some questions that never go away. It's not enough
to have loved Jesus yesterday; do I love him today? This
is one area where we evangelicals fail. We have a
tradition of instant conversions, in which a person's
eternal destiny turns on the decision of a moment. Now,
I certainly don't want to decry that (I made just such a
'decision' myself), even though recent surveys show that
most Christians are actually converted over a period of
time. Influenced by the mentality of the push-button
society we inhabit, however, we tend to press the logic
of the instant conversion into other areas. Our salvation
is secure because of a one-off commitment we made a
while ago; if, in practice, we backslide, we can always
'come back to the Lord' by 'rededicating' ourselves and
walking down to the front of a meeting in tears at an
altar call made for the purpose. And then everything
really will be all right, won't it? Until the next time.
Entire sanctification, filling with the Holy Spirit, 'em-
powerment for service': all of these things have been
held, at some time or another in recent Christian history,
to be attainable in one fell swoop as the result of 'laying
it all on the altar', or some such single dramatic decision
by you or me. We observe with joy that God sometimes
heals people of illnesses, but then we carry this over into
the realms of social, psychological and spiritual problems of all kinds, and assume that these, too, should
normally be 'claimed by faith' in a one-off prayer session or 'act of deliverance'. We are into what can only be
described as 'shazzam' mode. Wam! Kerpow! It will
happen!

This way of proceeding is not only much quicker than
long drawn out processes of encouragement, discipleship, healing and tender loving care; it is much less
costly as well. I will leave aside the point that it is also,
by and large, much less effective, leaving many people
frustrated and feeling condemned for their supposed
lack of faith. For my point here is that there are very
many issues which cannot simply be answered once and
for all and then considered as settled. Such a proposition

may be true for Jesus' dealing with our sins upon the cross, but the same cannot be said for the things that we do. For us, there are many questions that will never go away. Our Christian life consists in answering them— not once, but constantly—with 'Yes, Lord'.

Jesus told the disciples that, 'if anyone would come after me, he must deny himself and take up his cross daily and follow me' (Lk.9.23). It is not enough to take it up once for, unless today brings me literal martyrdom, I am still here tomorrow. And Jesus is still interested in what I shall do then. This is why we are to be 'living sacrifices' (Rom.12.1). Paul, observing that he and his companions were endangering themselves 'every hour', added 'I die every day' (1 Cor.15.30–31). At every moment of every day the question comes to us, 'Will you take up your cross in this situation?' It is a question which is always being answered, and yet which is never answered.

The same is true of relations amongst ourselves. Someone does me a great wrong, and I forgive them. I may really mean it, but then am surprised to find myself feeling resentful towards them a few days later, and 'freezing them out' of conversation. Perhaps the situation will continue for a while until we finally get together and talk it out 'man-to-man'. We are reconciled amidst hugs and tears. But then I do the same thing again. The truth is, I need to forgive my friend every day. Every day I must lay down the grudge which I have 'every right' to bear against him.

The same thing is true of our marriages. At our wedding, I told my wife I would love her 'until death us do part'. But that's precious little comfort to her today if, in fact, I mistreat her or neglect her, or run away with somebody else. Will I love her today, now, this minute? It's a decision I have to go on making.

In a way, Peter was extraordinarily privileged to be subjected to such bizarre treatment as to have the same question fired at him three times in quick succession. Imagine having to answer the same question, if only

within the precincts of your own mind, several times
during the course of an ordinary conversation. Would
your words or your thoughts turn to gossip, scandal,
anger, envy, if every few seconds you were having to
turn to the Lord and say, 'Yes, I love you'? Somehow, I
doubt it. And what Jesus keeps asking Peter, he keeps
asking us all.

There is one final point to be made about these
nagging questions that refuse to go away: they leave us
full of self-doubt. Because of them, I am never finally
persuaded about the propriety of my own motives; I am
constantly keeping an eye on the infinite deceptiveness
of my own heart. In the narcissistic culture which we
inhabit, however, we are taught that self-doubt is a bad
thing. Salesmen, politicians, corporate managers, 'experts' of one kind or another: all exude a calm, smiling
self-assurance. In most professions, success is obtained
by fostering an illusion of competence and trading on
the other person's insecurities. (Advertising is about
little else: 'No one will notice you without X'; 'If you
really care for your kids you'll buy them Y'; 'Assure
your future with our pension plan'.)

In the church we spiritualize the same impulses. Of
course, we criticize the smoothness and falsity of the
shallow self-assuredness in these secular figures: that is
hardly a difficult exercise. But then we set up Christian
counter-examples of exactly the same thing. 'Real assur-
ance', we tell the world in round, smooth tones, 'comes
from knowing Jesus', and hope we are believed, before
going home to less-than-ideal domestic situations and
the ever-present struggle with our own temptations.
And because we 'ordinary Christians' know we're like
this, we then project *real* competence onto our leaders.
The good preacher is the authoritative figure who can
convince us that he *knows*, that he's got it all together
and can show us just how to sort our lives out; we go to
camps and events in which Christian celebrities give us
breezy seminars on making our youth work really effective (like, say, a church we have read about in a book) or

improving our evangelistic strategy in three easy stages. Once again, it's all a myth. The illusion of competence is precisely that: an illusion. Not only do our leaders not have all the answers, they have not even sorted themselves out. Every now and again, one of them will run off with their secretary—how many do you think are struggling with problems on a much lower level without ever reaching such a crisis point? Why do we insist on telling one another that Christianity is an automatic path to strength and wholeness (if only we have enough faith!), when we know from the charts that God's power 'is made perfect in weakness' (2 Cor.12.9)?

I would go so far as to say that, far from being a *dis*qualification, self-doubt is actually a qualification for service and ministry. Only when I know that I *haven't* got everything sorted out am I forced to rely upon the power of God. Twice recently I have caught myself trying to encourage nervous people who were just beginning on public teaching ministries with the consoling words, 'Go on, you can do it: I believe in you.' I now realize that 'I believe in you' can never be more than a merely social encouragement, a sort of equivalent to the much more realistic, 'Come on; I'm with you in this.' It may sound fine, but the implication is that, if I 'believe in them', then so should they. And frankly, the world— let alone the church—could do without two more people who 'believe in themselves'. In any case, the truth is, I don't even believe in myself; Paul's dictum that 'in my flesh dwelleth no good thing' (Rom.7.18 AV) is more than a doctrine to which I must give intellectual assent; rather, it is an experiential reality. And if I don't believe in me, whom I know, why should I believe in them? Probably only because I cannot see into the depths of their hearts. Their ministry will be much more effective if, instead, they believe in God, who lifts up the downcast and exalts the humble.

And what if I say that my heart is wracked by temptations and ambiguities, and my mind riddled with uncertainties and doubts? The most famous Christian leaders in the world would be forced to admit the same, if only in the quietness of their own consciences. So there is no need for me to put up an illusion of something that simply isn't true. The maintaining of illusions demands distance and, if I wish to play that game, I will be forced to keep the very lambs I claim to be feeding at arm's length, in case they discern the reality. Only if I acknowledge my own weakness and self-doubts will my ministry point people towards Jesus and away from me. That is because self-doubt forces us, having done all, not to rely upon that all, knowing as we do its insufficiency, but instead to cast ourselves upon God. We are compelled to stand aside and let him act.

The conclusion we have reached is not tantamount to mysticism, or even to asceticism. The idea that the self must in some sense be destroyed before we can be used by God is to deny the goodness of God's creation and ourselves as created in his image. God does not despise our createdness or our individuality. On the contrary: he wishes to use them. The real, undeluded self needs to be submitted—not destroyed—so that the cliché about 'Jesus shining through us' becomes a reality, instead of so many hollow words. The Old Testament prophets, the New Testament apostles, men and women throughout the history of the church and in its life today have been, and are, used by God to diffract the light of his life and his love through an infinite variety of personal and cultural variables. In the same way, he wants to 'shine' through me, but then I can be under no illusions about who 'I' am, or ministering Jesus will quickly become confused with self-promotion. In this way, I am trusting God to meet people's needs through me, *in spite* of who I am and *because* of who he is.

The scene by the fire in the high priest's courtyard had delivered Peter from his delusions about the reality of his own love for Jesus; the repeated question would never allow him to become deluded again. And yet the

question's insistence, whilst undermining Peter's cocki-
ness, affirms, at the same moment, his value. By constantly wanting to hear Peter say, 'I love you, Lord',
Jesus is letting Peter know how much he matters to him.
It is my wife whom I want to hear saying to me 'I love
you'—not once, or even once a day, but several times a
day. Am I megalomanic? No; it's just that her love
means that much to me. And Peter's love means that
much to Jesus. So does yours. So does mine. In the very
act of puncturing our self-assurance by reminding us of
the murk within, he reaffirms our value and his love for
us.

Jesus' insistent 'Do you love me?' is a question that is
never finally answered; it will confront me constantly
until I see him in heaven. Until then, it remains both a
nagging doubt about my own good faith, and a reassurance of his. Which is just exactly why Jesus keeps asking
it.

THREE

The Price

Jesus said, 'Feed my sheep. I tell you the truth, when you were younger you dressed yourself and went where you wanted; but when you are old you will stretch out your hands, and someone else will dress you and lead you where you do not want to go.' Jesus said this to indicate the kind of death by which Peter would glorify God. Then he said to him, 'Follow me!'
Peter turned and saw that the disciple whom Jesus loved was following them. ... When Peter saw him, he asked, 'Lord, what about him?'
Jesus answered, 'If I want him to remain alive until I return, what is that to you? You must follow me' (Jn.21.17-22).

It is only after Jesus has asked Peter if he loves him, and after he has told him, three times, to feed his lambs, that he tells Peter the true cost of fulfilling his ministry. 'I tell you the truth,' he says, 'when you were younger you dressed yourself and went where you wanted; but when you are old you will stretch out your hands, and someone else will dress you and lead you where you do not want to go' (Jn.21.18). Peter was to end his days in Rome as a martyr for Jesus, one of many Christians put to death by the emperor Nero in the aftermath of the Great

Fire of Rome in 64 AD. Tradition has it that he was crucified, possibly upside down. John's gospel was not written until after these events, probably sometime in the last two decades of the first century, and so, after quoting Jesus' words to Peter, John felt able to add, 'Jesus said this to indicate the kind of death by which Peter would glorify God' (v.19). John's readers already knew about Peter's crucifixion, and so no explanation of the significance of 'stretching out your hands' would have been needed.

Living in a Western country in the 1990s, the prospect of martyrdom seems like an unreal possibility—relevant to other times and places, perhaps, but for you and me right now simply the stuff of vainglorious fantasies. Perhaps we shouldn't be so sure. More people have died for Christ in this century than in any other. In some of the countries of west Africa in recent years, Muslims have carried out massacres of their fellow-citizens specifically for being Christians. Most of us are familiar with the persecution of Christians under the various Communist régimes of eastern Europe, China and elsewhere, and most of us are generally aware of the severe persecution that continues to face the small underground churches of the Muslim world, even if the very nature of those churches precludes most of us from knowing details, or of divulging them if we do. Faraway countries of which we know little? We forget that, even in Britain, religious dissenters have enjoyed freedom from official persecution only since 1689; just over 300 years, or barely fifteen per cent of the time since Jesus and Peter had their chat on the beach by the lake. And ways were found, even after 1689, to make life difficult for those who wished to follow Jesus outside of 'officially approved' channels. Most countries have enjoyed unfettered liberty for the gospel for even less time, and the majority of governments still do not grant it.

Could persecution return here? If one means, 'Will Christians be imprisoned and put to death for preaching the gospel?' then the answer must be, 'Probably not.'

But how will we handle something far less dramatic (or, for the fantasizers, less melodramatic)? One does not need to be a political arch-conservative to see that, in Western countries, the rising tide of 'political correctness' is likely to restrict the extent to which Christians will, in future, be permitted to express their beliefs in absolute truth and absolute moral values. How far will we compromise our opinions and our practices, and the way we express these, in order not to harm our career prospects or our education? It's true, you don't have to work on Sundays, but don't expect to be taken on in a new job if you won't. Certainly, Christian nurse or doctor, you don't have to take part in abortions, but don't expect to be employed in gynæcology or ante-natal care. (And two of the three main political parties will not allow you to stand as a candidate for them if you wish to restrict the abortion laws.) Of course you don't have to watch TV programmes, listen to radio programmes, or read newspapers with sexually sugges-tive material—you can always switch off or stop buying. It's just that that will leave you watching sport and reading the *Beano*. (I exaggerate, of course—but not much!) Already one large church in south London has, for more than a decade, experienced constant harass-ment from its local authority (including attempts to prevent initiatives to help the unemployed and to pro-vide laundry services in areas where such services had been closed down by vandals), because the church's leader is on record as insisting that the practice of homosexuality is a sin. It is not fanciful, or preachers' heady rhetoric, to suggest that pressure on Christian churches, church leaders, Christian companies and or-ganizations, and on Christians themselves, to weaken and give way on their attempts to uphold truth and righteousness, to say the shibboleths of the postmodern West, is going to intensify greatly over the next two or three decades. No one is going to be hanged, drawn and quartered. No one is going to be shot at dawn. There will just be the relentless pressure to capitulate in all kinds of areas of morality, with serious consequences for one's career or education, or ability to run one's church or Christian organization or company, if one does not. What will you do? What will I do? Because Jesus wants to know.

My fear is that the changes coming in the West will cloud the whole issue. We will tend to give in because the thing that society is requiring us to retract doesn't seem to be 'the central point of the gospel', and the penalty for failing to comply doesn't seem so ultimate either. Let us not deceive ourselves. Our brothers and sisters under the Communist régimes were only rarely put to death simply for being Christians. More usually, they were deprived of decent housing, or a decent job, or a proper education. Restrictions were placed on Sunday schools, and upon who could be baptized, pastors had to be approved by government, the content of sermons was regulated, evangelism was restricted to church buildings. Always the point at issue was less than ultimate, and the penalty less than immediate 'death for Jesus'.

Even during the Reformation, the vast majority of those who were burned during the reign of the Catholic Queen Mary did not suffer for refusing to recant their belief in justification by faith, or their trust in the Bible, or even their rejection of the authority of the pope. No—all the pressure was applied elsewhere: they were required to affirm belief in the Catholic doctrine of transubstantiation, that is, the belief that the bread and wine in communion literally become the body and blood of Christ. A wrongheaded belief, perhaps, from a Protestant viewpoint, but . . . something to die for? Why not accept? After all, one could still keep one's other, arguably more important, beliefs intact. But most chose to die rather than subscribe to this doctrine. Even in the early church, when the Christians were being persecuted by the Romans, not all persecutions entailed the demand to give up being a Christian. On some occasions, Christians were required to surrender their copies of the Scriptures to the authorities. Surely, more copies could have been made later? All the same, many died rather than give in.

It seems strange, but the big sacrifices tend to be easier to make than the small ones. There came a point in our life together when my wife and I had to make a decision about our future direction in discipleship and ministry. The Lord was calling us in a direction which, if we obeyed, would cost us all of the money, including the stake in our house, that we had. It would leave us poor, certainly for a number of years, and perhaps permanently, and there were no guarantees, humanly speaking, of what would happen on the other side of the jump. Of course, we needed to think and pray about it long and hard but, in the end, we jumped. I don't feel particularly proud about getting 'the big one' right; there are countless far smaller sacrifices which God is calling me to make, day by day, which I fail to heed. After all, how is one more sinful thought going to hurt? Does one more little piece of selfishness really count that much?

It is the same with persecution. Most of the Christians that I know, and most of those reading this book, if asked 'Would you die rather than renounce your faith in Christ?' would, I suspect, answer 'Yes'. I have my doubts whether all of us, if it really were to come to that, would actually do so. But that is not quite my point here. We say we're prepared to die for Christ, but in practice we're not prepared to live for him. We are not prepared to be 'living sacrifices' (Rom.12.1). We stand ready to lay down our lives, but when called upon by the mundane, inglorious and utterly unromantic circumstances of every day to lay down, moment by moment, the trivia which in their totality go to make up what we call 'our lives', we cannot or, at any rate, we will not. We think we would be prepared to pay 'in a lump', but in practice we will not pay piecemeal. Isn't this paradoxical? Like Simon Peter, we fail to deliver on what we promise!

Up until recently, I've believed that, when the chips are down, martyrdom is something we shouldn't hesitate to embrace, although we shouldn't go courting it either. But increasingly I'm beginning to see that we may be called upon to act in ways which provoke just such a result. Jesus calls us to fly in the teeth of opposition, regarding our lives as of little account. Eugene Peterson's paraphrase of the apostle Paul's words on this subject expresses the idea beautifully:

> Alive, I'm Christ's messenger; dead, I'm his bounty. Life versus even more life. I can't lose.
> As long as I'm alive in this body, there is good work for me to do. If I had to choose right now, I hardly know which I'd choose. Hard choice! The desire to break camp here and be with Christ is powerful. Some days I can think of nothing better (Phil.1.22–23 in E.Peterson, *The Message*).

Perhaps that's the attitude that needs to be in us: 'Do what you want, world; it doesn't matter.' Most of us, realistically, are unlikely to be put to death for our faith, barring drastic changes. But all of us are called upon to live moment by moment in such a way—developing attitudes of heart and mind—that, if and when *that moment* were to come, we would be prepared. We will have a settled confidence 'that Christ will be exalted in my body, whether by life or by death' (Phil.1.20), and that God's grace will be sufficient for the eventuality.

Despite all of his previous failures, Jesus had enough confidence in Peter's commitment to let him in on the secret of the terrible price he would have to pay for feeding Jesus' sheep. How far are we prepared to go? Are we prepared to tell God, 'Do whatever it takes for the image of your Son to be formed in me, to make me all that you want me to be: I'm willing to pay the price'? And if we're not willing to pray such a prayer—and the extent of my own conviction on the subject has been known to vary—can we at least pray, 'Lord, *make me willing* to pay the price'?

What About Him?

A Puritan has been defined as a person with an obsessive fear that someone, somewhere might be enjoying themselves. Well, most of us tend to have a similar fear that somebody, somewhere might be enjoying more of God's blessing than *me*. When it comes to ministry, we are afraid that someone else's ministry is more appreciated than mine. Let's not exaggerate: perhaps we preachers know it's unrealistic to aspire to be another Billy Graham, perhaps the counsellors know they can't be Jay Adams, maybe the healers don't really expect to be another John Wimber . . . but we're certainly going to make sure that we're at the top in our own fellowship or Christian organization!

Now all of this raises an interesting question: do we want to be the hero of the sheep, or to feed them? If the latter, why do we spend so much time looking over our shoulders in case someone else's ministry, some other brother's Sunday school lessons, someone else's sermons, the other sister's counselling, are more appreciated than mine? To want to do our best is not only legitimate, it's positively praiseworthy; our trouble too often is that we want our ministries to be *relatively* the best (relative, that is, to others engaged in serving Jesus), and that's a different story. Who are we doing this for? I mean really?

Peter has been talking to Jesus, and has just been told some unwelcome news about the consequences for him personally of feeding Jesus' lambs. Now he turns around to find that John has been following them. (Maybe John had been listening in on the conversation after all!) And of course, Peter wants to know if the same delightful prospects are in store for this other brother. Because if they are, then perhaps being martyred won't be so bad—especially if it's not due to happen until he's old anyway. Even apparent failure or rejection is OK, as long as those around us have to face it too!

What conditions do we want to make for exercising a ministry? That it be successful? That we are appreciated? Do I feel blessed by God only when other people appreciate me? Who am I really working for?

Too many of us want our rewards for feeding Jesus' sheep now. Never mind rewards in heaven—tell me *now* what a great job I'm doing! The really sad thing about all of this is not simply that we want them; that merely betrays our lack of faith in the promises of the very Jesus whom we claim to be serving. No, the real tragedy is that many of us actually get what we want. Mostly we set up our 'ministries' in such a way as to yield maximum adulation (but that is something we shall examine in a later chapter). If only we could see our ministries in true, heavenly perspective, we would change our approach. If Satan wishes to tempt me to despair, his line of approach is along a road that too many of us have left wide open for him: 'Meic, you've got everything you want in this life; in the story of Dives and Lazarus, it's clear which one is closer to you—you've *had* your good things.' And 'Serving God? Really? and everyone says, "hey, Meic, that was a good talk" [well, there was someone once!]. You're just like the Pharisees praying on the street corners; Jesus said that they've *had* their reward in full. You don't think there'll be rewards in heaven for it too, do you?' And of course, as with all of Satan's temptations, he has a point.

We need to get it firmly fixed into our heads that there are few Brownie points for being a hero in front of the sheep; they are given for serving. I get to preach a lot, and I've been made aware by sheer experience that there are very few rewards in heaven which have been earned in the pulpit (except perhaps when addressing a hostile mob!). Most of the time, being given the privilege of sharing with people from the word of God is, in the very best sense, its own reward. But the rewards in heaven are earned by witnessing to people in danger or under stress, by unheroic deeds like visiting the sick and the lonely, by time spent in secret with Jesus, by anonymous good deeds where the right hand doesn't know what the left hand is doing. 'And your Father,' says Jesus, 'who sees what is done in secret, will reward you' (Matt.6.18). Sometimes I wonder: do we believe all this stuff?

Perhaps I might anticipate a possible misunderstanding at this point. I certainly am not saying that we should refrain from encouraging others in their ministries for fear that 'they will lose their rewards in heaven'. That would be ridiculous! We need to be more supportive, and more encouraging, of one another, not less. But then I'm not talking here about our attitudes towards one another's ministries at all, but about our attitudes towards our own.

On what does my security depend? Do I get my self-image from the fact that God has settled his love upon me and sent his Son to die for me? Or do I seek it in the appreciation of others for 'fulfilling my ministry'— which is just another way of saying that I am merely doing what he has called me to do? Do I feel good because I know and am experiencing God's care? Do I get it from the way outward circumstances are looking right now? If my security is really in God, then I am secure indeed. If it rests in whether or not other people appreciate me and 'my ministry', then I will constantly be seeking to bolster my position in the fellowship where I am by a thousand and one subtle, or not-so-subtle, devices that have nothing to do with serving Jesus or my brothers and sisters. Sadly, I would have to contend that, most of the time, we follow the latter course, with devastating effects upon our own spiritual lives and those of our churches. 'What is that to you?' Jesus asks Peter. For most of us, the answer would be, 'A heck of a lot'.

What Peter is told, in effect, is this: 'The response to your ministry will be that some people will want to crucify you. And they will. But John will continue to live, and have several decades more of fruitful ministry. He will write New Testament books more important than yours—and in better Greek!—that will still be read two thousand years from now. How do you feel about that, Peter? Do you still love me? Good—then feed my lambs. If the other guy remains until I come again, that's nothing to you. You follow me.'

It's interesting, isn't it, that the command to 'Follow me' is the first thing Jesus is recorded as telling Peter (Matt.1.18–19), as well as the last. It's the same for us: the call to follow, regardless of consequences, is Jesus' first word, and his last. Do we love him? Will we do what he says, whatever the price? Because nothing else matters.

PART II

The Authority Obsession

FOUR

Worldly Powers

In the horrifying war in the Balkans, some forces have earned a particularly sinister reputation. These are the irregular militias who have massacred, raped and ethnically cleansed their way across large stretches of Bosnia and Croatia. Everywhere, they have spread misery and terror on a scale which has not been seen in Europe since 1945, as part of their campaign to create, say, a greater Serbia. As with Churchill's famous V-for-victory sign in the Second World War, the Četnik forces have a morale-raising gesture which they make to one another, by raising the thumb and first two forefingers. The three digits stand for Father, Son, and Holy Spirit. For these people identify the cause of the nation with Christianity in the form of the Serbian Orthodox Church. Their enemies, Catholic Croats and Bosnian Muslims, are seen as God's enemies, and so no cruelty is too great to be used against them.

Young men in former Yugoslavia are incited by propaganda, propelled by fear of their fellows, caught up in a spiral of events and the 'need to obey orders', to perpetrate acts of violence, degradation and brutality. When they have done these things once, it becomes much

41

easier to do them again. The need to justify these actions to themselves, along with the supportive approval of their peers and senior officers, causes them in the end to take pleasure in them. Within a few months they come to relish actions which they would previously have looked upon with horror.

From my own visits to the region, I have witnessed at first hand the destruction, hatred and bitterness which have been engendered. Once it gets started, it becomes a self-perpetuating process. Amongst those who have witnessed the shelling of their cities, the loss of loved ones and the influx of terrified refugees, the bitterness runs deep. So much is easily understandable. But the hostility goes further than that. The desire of the victims to have revenge, even at the cost of more casualties to themselves, is universal. Perfectly intelligent, educated people believe the most improbable conspiracy theories about the other side: 'They've been planning this since the Second World War' is one that I heard. What? Millions of people put together a massacre strategy? Secretly? Over decades?

What is it that divides these people? What makes them perceive one another as different at all? They're all the same colour, and they all speak a language we used to call Serbo-Croat. Admittedly the Serbs use the Eastern Cyrillic alphabet to write it down, whilst the Croats use the Western Roman script. So has all the killing been about an alphabet? The other major difference is, of course, religion. Admittedly, not all would say they were fighting for religion, and in many cases religious zeal was created by the conflict rather than bringing the fighting about in the first place. But all three communities have, to a very significant degree, been shaped by their respective religions. Catholicism has shaped the culture of what it means to be a Croat; it has penetrated the very warp and weft of life, so to speak. Orthodoxy has done the same for the Serbs, and Islam, however moderate, for the Bosnians. Not unreasonably, these nations define themselves in terms of religion.

Something very similar was true of mediæval Europe in general. If we could have spoken to a thirteenth-century English peasant (Baldrick, for instance) and asked him, 'What kind of a human being are you?', he very likely would not have called himself English (or even a peasant) at all. He would have identified himself first and foremost as a Christian, and then as the subject of a particular lord (Blackadder). By being a Christian he would not have meant what we mean—namely that he had a personal faith, or had experienced a conversion. Being 'Christian' meant being a Western European, and *not* a Muslim, like the Turks. His identification of his society would have been a religious one, for religion determined and justified the shape of that society, its structure and social order and, above all, its distribution of power. That is something that all 'pre-moderns' understand instinctively, and something that modern Westerners fail to comprehend. That is why the crusaders could weep with tears of joy as they waded through the blood of Muslims and Jews in the streets of Jerusalem; the triumph of their culture was the triumph of God. People in Northern Ireland understand this still. The conflict there has not been simply about religion, but about power and the character and culture of society which religion both reflects and creates. That is why so many outsiders have found it impossible to empathize with such a depth of feeling, and have tended to write off the entire population of the province as mad. Most Westerners tend to do the same in the case of Middle Eastern Muslims. Our failure to understand it at all simply reveals how parochial we westerners are. We think of ourselves as so cosmopolitan, but this is a bad joke: we can get along with anyone, from any part of the world . . . as long as they're Westernized cosmopolitans like us!

Let us leave aside this particular instance of the many absurdities of the Western worldview. Wearing our Christian 'hat', rather than our Western one, we can at least console ourselves that we are right to reject the

'traditional' view of the role of religion, as espoused in
the Balkans, or by the crusaders. Such a view is anath-
ema to the evangelical understanding of what Christianity is all about. The community which Jesus calls
together is not about power, in a political, human sense,
at all. He is calling disciples out of the world, not
creating a structure to govern it.

But in rejecting state religion and its misuse down the
ages, we have nothing to be complacent about. The fact
is that we frequently misuse Christian ideas, church
structures and, especially, 'ministries' as platforms for
power. Even if we do not aim at world or state-
domination, we all too frequently dress up the desire to
control and manipulate other individuals, or even entire
congregations, in spiritual-sounding language.

This kind of behaviour is so all-pervasive that it is
difficult to know where to begin in quoting examples.
Perhaps it will seem less threatening if I start by mentioning an uncomfortable aspect of the history of that
part of the body with which I identify, namely the 'new
churches' (or what used to be called the 'house
churches'). Not so long ago, many of these had a de-
served reputation for authoritarianism. As a young
Christian, I was present at the early conferences and
Bible weeks in the 1970s which marked the upsurge in
the growth of the movement. A generation of Christian
young people—my generation—were presented with
what seemed to us a whole new vision of what the
church could be: the use of the gifts of the Holy Spirit
would lead to every member participating and ministering in church, the body of Christ would build itself up in
love as it was strengthened by 'that which every joint
supplied', until we all attained to unity in the faith. It
sounded so right. And I still think it does. The denominations were derided—for their narrowness, for their
clergy-laity split, for their one-man leadership. How we
laughed and cheered as we recognized ourselves and
our home churches in the caricatures that were drawn

from the platform. These men had got it right; we would follow.

The sequel was less satisfactory. It seemed to me then, and it seems still, that, having gained a following on the basis of these ideas, the leaders immediately erected fences around their followers, forbade meaningful and genuinely open fellowship with other Christians, and turned their networks of congregations into outfits that were at least as denominational in spirit as the churches that people had just left. The analogy is an absurd one, since I was a person with no influence upon events, but I felt like a sort of Trotsky figure to the leaders' Stalin: the revolution had been betrayed! The whole episode reminds me of Henry Nevinson's definition of 'chivalry': 'releasing beautiful maidens from other men's castles and taking them to your own castle'.

The horror stories that were circulated about the degree of submission to leaders that was expected of members may have been largely untrue, but there was at least some substance in the accusations. Frequently, leaders dominated the lives and dictated the life-decisions of those they were supposedly serving, and always the justifications given sounded so spiritual, and so persuasive. One should not attend the meetings of other Christians—because the sheep had to be protected from outside preachers and others who were accountable to no one but themselves (or who were not accountable, at any rate, to the leaders of the house churches). Tithing to the church was clearly right—it was a practice with some tradition behind it, and if leaders could not be trusted to use the money wisely, what was the point of submitting to their authority at all? (Even so, it soon became obvious that, in the new parlance, an 'apostle' was a preacher with a Mercedes!) Because churches should be local (to facilitate evangelizing an area), members should be strongly encouraged to live close to the meeting-place. (It also had the merit of making it easier to check up on members.) Most single people go through several 'relationships' before meeting the person they want to marry and so, to avoid the disruption and heartache this causes, elders would decide whether a given couple were suitable to be boyfriend-and-girlfriend. (I once had to be given the 'all-clear' by the elder of another church before I could date one of 'his' young people. Even so, the relationship lasted only five months!)

Each individual was supposedly being discipled by someone 'over them in the Lord'. Such authority was meant to be built upon genuine relationship, it was clearly for the disciple's benefit and growth, and there were texts which could be pressed into service to provide scriptural authority for the practice. Moreover, each discipler was himself being discipled in turn by his own discipler. Logically, this would have led to a sort of evangelical pope at the head of each network of churches. However, we were assured that, at that level in the spiritual stratosphere, the apostles and prophets 'covered one another'.

I was—and am—grateful that our own church remained aloof from the various pyramid structures of this type that were erected during the late 1970s and early '80s. A few years ago, when it had become clear that the original revolution, once betrayed, had very definitely become *un*betrayed once more, the congregation consented to join one of the networks of what by now were known as 'new churches'. Since the mid-1970s, many of the denominational churches have quietly and unostentatiously adopted a whole range of the medicines prescribed for them in those early Bible weeks concerning worship styles, spiritual gifts, plural leadership and other matters. But on the 'shepherding' issue, it is the new churches which have responded to withering criticism and changed their position. Some, of course, had never been down this road in the first place. Others had done so to differing degrees. The road of retreat has been travelled at different paces as well. But almost all have now rejoined the mainstream of church life.

It is simply no good, however, for others—whether critics within the house churches, like myself, or those outside—to pretend that the issues thus highlighted have nothing to do with them. On the contrary, these events merely throw into sharp relief something that most of us do with our own ministries most of the time. In those house churches that went down the authoritarian route for a while, 'Submit to your leaders!' was a cry that came, by and large, from the leaders, or from those who hoped that, if they were conspicuously loyal enough for long enough, they soon would be leaders, regardless of whether or not they had any other giftings for such a role. All too often the declamation, 'What this church needs is more teaching!', can be translated as, 'I fancy myself as a preacher'. 'What we need is real worship', especially coming from a worship leader, can be a demand for more space, more prominence. Pleas to emphasize children's work in the congregation tend to come from the Sunday school leaders. In a hundred different ways, we seek to get our churches to play to *our* strengths, and thus to enhance our own positions. One current American commentator, interviewing disaffected Christians who have given up on church, concludes that the reason most sermons fail to connect with the people to whom they are delivered is that, however clever or incisive or well-constructed they might be, most function psychologically to enhance the reputation of the preacher, and the preacher's influence over the congregation, rather than seeking to lead people to an encounter with God for themselves. That may not be the conscious intention of the preacher, but it is the all-too-frequent effect. The same thing might be said of much that passes as 'ministry'.

Even our one-to-one relationships are not immune to the same poison. Perhaps I express spiritual disapproval of something that you're doing (perhaps quite legitimately so), and tell you that I'll pray for you; but the whole nature of this exchange between us can also be used to let you know that I'm more spiritually mature than you, and have a senior standing in the Christian community—and that you'd better not forget it. Perhaps you and your friends are intimidated by the obvious extent of her Christian experience and gifting in children's work, but she's only just moved into the area and so is new to this congregation. So when the classes are re-assigned, you tell her that the committee had asked the Lord to give them a list of who should be doing this work . . . and her name just wasn't on the list that the Lord gave. A Christian woman has a backslidden husband; she complains to the folks in church about the difficulties this causes her, and they sympathize. They look down on him, and rather fear him as an ogre in the path of their sister's discipleship. And that, she feels, pays him back nicely for all the minor irritations around the house, and gives her the moral highground in the usual petty domestic warfare over socks and toothpaste and who did the vacuuming last.

Too many of us who claim to be building the kingdom of God, and using rhetoric about enthroning Jesus, have our calf and ankle twisted around a leg of that throne, and are quietly trying to shuffle it under our own behinds. We speak of the powers of the age to come, but finish by using them in the service of worldly powers.

FIVE

The Harvest and the Harvesters

After this the Lord appointed seventy-two others and sent them two by two ahead of him to every town and place where he was about to go. He told them, 'The harvest is plentiful, but the workers are few. Ask the Lord of the harvest, therefore, to send out workers into his harvest field. Go! I am sending you out like lambs among wolves. Do not take a purse or bag or sandals; and do not greet anyone on the road' (Lk.10.1–4).

Job Satisfaction?

Jesus does not supply harvest fields of ministry in order to help his disciples feel fulfilled by labouring in them. On the contrary, Jesus sees a world full of need, likens it to a harvest field, and *consequently* calls upon his disciples to go and work in them. But we postmodern Westerners tend to put the self first: I have a need to do something—or to *feel* that I'm doing something; I need to be needed; I need an outlet for my abilities. Fulfilling a ministry will provide all of this. This is the opposite of Jesus' priorities.

49

'But wait a minute', someone will object. 'You think that all Christians are involved in ministry of some kind. Surely you yourself believe—even hope—that Christians will find fulfilment as they exercise their ministries and serve the body of Christ?' Certainly. I myself find immense satisfaction in the work that the Lord has given me to do. But if finding personal satisfaction is our aim in 'ministering', then we do not come to serve Jesus, for really we are serving ourselves. 'Seek first his kingdom and his righteousness', says Jesus, 'and all these things'—our human wants—'will be given to you as well' (Matt.6.33). If our own satisfaction is our real target, however, then we know what to do: go for it, and it alone, for we cannot serve God and mammon. Paul warned Timothy about those who thought that godliness was a means to personal profit. 'Godliness with contentment is great gain', he pointed out, but it wasn't the kind of gain that some thought: 'if we have food and clothing, we will be content with that' (1 Tim.6.5–8). To use the service of God as a means to one's own ends is not only to put the cart before the horse; it is actually self-contradictory. We have spent our lives living for ourselves and our own advantage; that is the very thing that Jesus has come to rescue us from. To try to make 'service of Jesus' a means to our own self-fulfilment is to attempt to subvert the purpose for which Jesus came and died—'that those who live should no longer live for themselves but for him who died for them and was raised again' (2 Cor.5.15)—and so to attempt the impossible.

Impossible or not, we still keep trying. C S Lewis, in his classic book *The Great Divorce*, portrays an imaginary day-trip to heaven by a number of people who do not like it when they get there. One woman, Pam, only wants to see her dead son Michael again. She is prepared to go through what she clearly sees as so much religious rigmarole if that is what is required to get into heaven to be with her boy. When she meets her own brother, and is assured by him that Michael is indeed in

heaven but cannot see her until she has learned to want
God for God's own sake, she is appalled. When it is
pointed out that she is trying to use God only as a
means to Michael, she starts to criticize God's morality:
he does not understand how high and holy an affection
maternal love is. In the end, what Pam calls her love for
her son stands exposed as an obsession, not so much
with Michael himself, as with her own feelings about
him, and her own grief at his early death. However right
he was to do so, Lewis knew he was treading on thin ice
in describing such an imaginary episode, but that is his
entire point: no goal, no aim, no matter how noble and
praiseworthy, can take precedence over wanting God for
God's own sake. Not because God is a megalomaniac,
but because any human aspiration, any love even, that
does not have its source and grounding in him is
poisoned at the root. It becomes, in the end, merely
another form of selfishness and self-gratification, no
matter with what high-sounding justifications it may
choose to dignify itself.

The issue is the same when we consider becoming a
Christian in the first place. We tend to focus on the fact
that the new believer will be assured of heaven. Again,
we put the cart before the horse. Jesus came to bring
heaven into sinners by transforming their lives; we are
more concerned to get sinners into heaven, with a little
repentance and a slightly enhanced morality as nice
optional extras. Jesus wants people who will follow him
for the sake of following him. When we obey, all kinds
of consequences and changes follow, and heaven is one
of those consequences. But if that is the only reason for
'committing our lives to Christ', then becoming a Christian is an entirely self-interested decision. Which is odd,
since Jesus has come precisely to call us away from lives
which have hitherto been spent in making self-
interested decisions. The evil of human self-interest is
what sent him to the cross in the first place. In calling a
person to become a Christian, Jesus does not ask 'Do

you want heaven?' for we all think that we do, but 'Will you follow me?'

So we come back to the question of the white fields. What was Jesus thinking of when he used the harvest fields as a simile? Why, people of course: our world is full of hungry, hurting people. People at war with one another. People at war with themselves. The sick and the lonely. People in the church and out of it who need to be listened to, taught, prayed with, given hospitality, loved. Children who need to hear about Jesus. Neighbours and others who are lost without him. Everywhere huge white fields! What does Jesus care about more: that you wade into this ocean of need, or the feelings you might have about yourself after you have? Well, what do you think?

Jesus tells his disciples to 'ask the Lord of the harvest . . . to send out workers into his harvest field', and then immediately follows this up with the command 'Go! I am sending you' (Lk.10.3). What is this? A cutting way of saying 'Be an answer to your own prayer'? A way of forestalling any attempt by us to say 'Here I am, Lord— send the other person'? Perhaps. Or maybe Jesus simply assumes that 'you'—his immediate hearers—will go, and is calling for prayer that God will touch others to do the same. Practically, it makes no difference. We must be amongst those who go; he is sending us. We must also be those who pray that God will send others.

Lambs Among Wolves

And how does he send us? To bind this, to loose that, to claim authority over the other thing? Well, perhaps. But first we must see the context, or we will misunderstand what Christian 'authority' means, and attempt to estab-lish our ministries upon the self-sufficient 'power-model' that is so much in vogue, and which we have borrowed from the world, even though Jesus says 'you are not to be like that' (Lk.22.26).

Not only does Jesus refuse to instil images of 'power' in his servants, he sends us out 'like lambs among wolves'. This is an image which it is impossible to reconcile with attempts to control or manipulate others using religious ideas as the means or justification. The period of so-called 'Christendom', as we have already said, saw one of the fullest expressions of this phenomenon, especially during the Middle Ages. Obey the king, the nobles, your landlord, the church authorities, because God says so. The feudal hierarchy is what God wants; indeed, there is a hierarchy just like it in heaven and the rest of the created order, going from God down to archangels, angels, people, and finally to animals and plants. The social hierarchy upon earth is a mirror of all of this, and so we can see that this is what God wants. (I seem to remember some of the early house-church leaders making similar arguments to justify their pyramids of authority.) In the Middle Ages, any attempt to change your place in life was seen as an attempt to violate the order of God. By the end of the Middle Ages, the religious rules and regulations concocted to control people's lives made the Pharisees' embellishments on the Law of Moses, about which Jesus had complained, seem trivial by comparison. But the Reformers—Luther, Zwingli, Calvin and the others—made no attempt to modify the basic social use that was made of religion, namely to regulate the daily life of every person living in a particular state. Like the Catholics, the Protestant leaders agreed in persecuting anyone who deviated from their 'official' churches in belief or practice, and so Protestants suffered in Catholic states and Catholics in Protestant ones. Each church denounced the others as wolves, and called its own adherents the sheep. They were certain that a 'wolf' meant simply 'heretic' or 'false teacher'. Each side was sure that their opponents were false teachers, and therefore the wolves, whilst they themselves were the true church. So in persecuting 'heretics' with fire and sword, they were protecting the

flock of Christ. Finally, the Anabaptists, who rejected the
whole idea of 'Christendom', and thought that churches
should consist only of personally committed disciples of
Jesus, devised a simple test for which was the 'true
church': when wolves and sheep come into contact with
one another, it is always the wolf which kills and the
sheep which are killed. There are no exceptions to this.
Since the Anabaptists were persecuted by everyone, and
persecuted no one, the simple explanation did tend to
put the issue in a clear light. This is not to imply, of
course, that *any* group which does not act aggressively
and is itself mistreated by others is therefore to be
identified with Jesus' lambs, for Satan can disguise
himself as an angel of light in this respect as in any
other. But those who are Jesus' lambs will meet this
criterion. Not all fruit are apples, but at least all apples
are fruit.

Those who are sent by Jesus to preach the gospel, to
heal the sick, to aid and comfort the suffering—in a
word, those who are called to feed his sheep—are sent
as lambs amongst wolves. They do not attempt to use
worldly power over others, for to do so is to adopt the
way of the wolf.

Yet the attempt to use spirituality to control or bully
others is well entrenched in the life of most of our
churches. I once asked a group of people from a wide
cross-section of churches whether any of them had
experience of the misuse of so-called 'personal prophecies'. These are apparent prophecies aimed at just
one individual, or a small group of individuals, telling
them 'you should do so-and-so', or 'the Lord says this to
you'. Now, personal prophecies are certainly not un-
biblical, and for many people they can be very helpful
and encouraging. But they are also extremely vulnerable
to abuse if they are given by a person who may not have
heard from the Lord in the first place, but may want to
steer someone in a particular direction, or simply to gain
a reputation as a highly spiritual individual who hears

clearly from God. Sometimes the would-be prophet will tell their victim whom they should marry or date (or cease dating), or to change their job, or move house etc., or tell them that they are to blame for some bad development in their lives. Whilst it is not impossible that God may wish to say any of these things to a person, the prophet needs to be on very sure ground indeed before delivering such a message. Unsurprisingly, few of them are, and the consequences can be distressing. Two surprising things emerged from my question to the group. In the first place, most of them had personal experience of such misuse, often of a hair-raising nature. Secondly and more hearteningly, all of them took it for granted, their own bad experiences notwithstanding, that God could and did act by giving prophecies to help and reassure his children. This was encouraging. In any case, Christians who believe that 'the gifts of the Spirit are for today' are far from having a monopoly on this kind of manipulative behaviour. One woman I know of, from a strongly non-charismatic background, was told that the very difficult birth of her child and the subsequent postnatal depression must be the result of unconfessed sin. The result, predictably, was a triumph for 'the accuser of the brethren', and she was driven deeper into depression than before.

The fact that so many Christians have experience of such attempts to manipulate others is a sad reflection on how many of our churches operate. One particular church known to me was virtually controlled by a group of people who thought of themselves as extremely spiritual, but in practice used sentences beginning 'Father says' (implying some special revelation) to short-cut sensible discussion on a whole range of issues in the life of the church. The others tended to feel intimidated, and mostly gave in to the pressure.

Other congregations are plagued by holy huddles of prayer and fellowship that—whether unthinkingly or deliberately—exclude certain individuals, especially newcomers. The tragedy is that such cliques, which all churches have, see themselves as particularly spiritual (because they are based upon prayer, building up intense relationships and so on), precisely when they are acting in an ungodly way. Cliques may be inevitable; all of us are drawn to some people more than to others. But if they are entirely closed, with no 'open ends', and if they dominate the more formal structures of church life—Sunday schools, prayer meetings, women's groups etc.—then those outside the established cliques are effectively excluded from any participation in the life of the church itself. This is not theoretical; it happens all of the time in most churches. I have seen these informal structures used as a means of what can only be called bullying those outside of them, with the 'insiders' claiming to be encouraging the 'outsiders' to conform to their idea of spiritual behaviour (which in fact amounted to a form of 'submission' to one forceful character in the group). In fact, this way of proceeding is the exact parallel of small children in school playing 'exclusion' games with one another in order to bully: 'Sophie and I are friends, and we won't play with you.' In school, it is always the new kid, or the foreigner, or the one unsure of himself, or the one with red hair or a lisp, or the girl whose abilities threaten the dominance of the existing leading light of the group, who is picked upon. And churches often operate the same way. One pastor's wife, who was supposedly overseeing the women's fellowship, effectively marginalized women of independent ideas or those she could not dominate. Not only were the sheep not fed, but many were driven away. To draw attention to these unedifying realities in our churches is very embarrassing, of course; a non-Christian psychologist would have a field-day with such an admission. But, as Christians, we are in the truth business, so it had better be said. We cannot act like wolves and expect to be counted by Jesus amongst his lambs, let alone amongst the shepherds.

Travelling Light?

After telling the seventy-two that he is sending them out
like lambs among wolves, Jesus then proceeds to give
them some very strange instructions. They are not to
take a purse, or a bag, or sandals, and they are not to
greet anyone on the road. What bizarre behaviour he
expects from his disciples! Clearly, Jesus was addressing
a specific situation, but these things are nevertheless
recorded for our instruction. So what are we to learn
from them? All of these strange prohibitions, which one
might have thought would make the disciples' task
needlessly difficult, have to do with the repudiation of
worldly power.

A purse is used for keeping money; but Jesus does not
want those who minister in his name to rely on their
calculation of what might be financially expedient. Some
of us are called to move into financially parlous situations in order to fulfil the ministry that Jesus is giving
us. It is not that money is of no consideration, but it
cannot be allowed to dictate Jesus' agenda in his disciples' lives and ministries. So when it comes to sending
out those who will go into the harvest, Jesus says 'Never
mind the purse.'

It is the same with the bag. A bag, of course, is used
for keeping things, for storage. Jesus does not want his
followers to rely simply on their own resources, for
these will always be insufficient. If we confine ourselves
to our own resources, we may see some success, but it
will always be less than what he wants to give us. Our
ministry will be dictated by our own estimates of what
we can achieve, based upon our resources and worldly
power. We will also become addicted to self-reliance,
finding it harder to trust Jesus alone for the future. So
Jesus says 'Never mind the bag either.'

The prohibition of sandals seems particularly strange.
Some commentators suggest that, since they will be able
to 'trample on snakes and scorpions' (v.19), they will not
need any kind of footwear. But in similar passages,

where Jesus gives instructions to the twelve before
sending them out (Matt. 10, Mk. 6, Lk. 9), he permits the
wearing of sandals and forbids the carrying of extra
clothing, so it may well be that it is only the carrying of
a second pair that he is discussing here. After all, he
speaks of not 'taking' sandals, rather than not 'wearing'
them. If so, then the sandals are like the bag; they count
as a sign that the disciple is self-reliant.

Finally we come to the oddest requirement of all. Why
in the name of reason should Jesus forbid his disciples
from greeting people that they pass on the road? After
all, he gives them elaborate instructions (vv.5–6) about
how they should greet those whose houses they enter.
Many scholars observe that Middle Eastern greetings
were long and elaborate, and speculate that the command to dispense with them reflects the urgency of the
disciples' task. But an alternative explanation is possible.
The greetings are symbolic, like the purse, the bag and
the sandals, of the attempt to rely upon worldly power.
In recent years we have become familiar with a new
verb: 'networking'. The term has nothing to do with
computers, but refers to the practice of ingratiating
ourselves with new people in key positions so that we
will be able to use them later for our own purposes. If
we have a wide network of well-placed acquaintances,
we feel powerful; indeed, we probably *are* powerful. In
Britain, the Christian subculture is still just small
enough—and the subcultures *within* the subculture are
certainly small enough—for most of us to have personal
acquaintance with some Christian celebrity, or well-
known preacher. Such contacts are often a matter of
pride. Before I took up my present job, I had few such
contacts, but at least I had some. Now, doing the work
that I do, I meet quite a lot of well-known people. Some
of them even remember my name from one meeting to
the next. Some of them even have such poor judgement
as to like me! As a result, I have noticed that one or two
of the 'folks back home' treat me . . . well, differently.
Why? Did I become someone different? Of course not;

I'm still the same little boy as before. But some of them can't help remembering: it's not what you know, but whom you know that counts!

And Jesus will have none of it. There is only one person we really need to know, and that's him. Which personal connections are we relying on—those with other people, or the one with him? Sadly, for most of us, time spent 'networking' exceeds time spent in secret with Jesus any day. So Jesus says, 'Never mind the networking.'

In all of these things, Jesus calls us decisively away from worldly power, and towards reliance upon him. It's not an easy thing to do; indeed, it feels strange and unnatural. That is because it is. But if we want to go into the harvest fields, helping to meet the ocean of need, we will find that it is the only basis for ministry. In wanting 'recognition' of our ministries and control over others, we want the reassurance of our own strength. But only a willingness to be weak can bring us the reassurance of *his* strength.

SIX

Whose Authority?

'He who listens to you listens to me; he who rejects you rejects me; but he who rejects me rejects him who sent me.'
The seventy-two returned with joy, and said, 'Lord, even the demons submit to us in your name.'
He replied, 'I saw Satan fall like lightning from heaven. I have given you authority to trample on snakes and scorpions, and to overcome all the power of the enemy; nothing will harm you. However, do not rejoice that the spirits submit to you, but rejoice that your names are written in heaven' (Lk.10.16–20).

It was a difficult interview. I had been asked to restrain someone whose 'words from the Lord' for various people around her were causing a problem. Like so much else that Sonia did, her revelations seemed designed to establish her 'spiritual superiority', and predictably she picked on people who were nervous, sensitive and none-too-self-assured to deliver them to. Finally, her actions caused serious distress to someone who had more than enough problems without the needless burden of worrying about whether or not to take this supposed missive from heaven seriously. It was important not to discourage others from continuing to use prophecy responsibly, but the time had clearly come to ask Sonia, at least, to desist altogether. I was not 'in faith' for her to accept correction, on this or any other point. And God honoured that faithlessness. As the conversation continued, she became quite annoyed, and began to bluster about the stamp of approval God had placed upon her purported ministry in this area. It became clear as she went on that, although she claimed to be defending her ministry and her message from God, she was actually defending herself.

Sonia had a point, though. According to Jesus' words in Luke 10, if Sonia's ministry really was from the Lord, then I was not merely restricting or rejecting her, but Jesus himself. It was necessary to be very sure indeed before taking such action. It is possible that I may be taken aside by the elders after preaching my next sermon, or receive remonstrating letters from readers of this book, for having taught false doctrine. Indeed, when preaching on one occasion on 'ministry' and related subjects, I observed one person in the congregation who was clearly 'praying against me'! (Don't ask me how I know they were, but I do!) Now in such a situation, there are only two possibilities. Either the person rejecting our ministry is in the right, in which case we need to accept the fact humbly and receive correction, or they are in the wrong, in which case they will answer to God for it, for 'he who rejects you rejects me'.

But either way, there is no need for us to get angry in our own defence. If we do, that is good evidence that it *is* ourselves that we are defending, and not 'the Lord's work'. On the one hand, Jesus assures us that those who receive our ministry are receiving it from the Lord himself—which should make us tremble at the magnitude of the responsibility placed upon us, and delight in the fact that he has chosen us to be channels of his grace to others. On the other hand, we do not have to worry if our ministry is rejected, for those who do so bring their own condemnation, without any assistance from us. The disciples are told simply to affirm that their ministry is from the Lord, to remove the dust of that town from their feet as a testimony, and to move on. No resistance. No embittered arguments. No defending of ourselves. If we are listened to, it is the Lord who is accepted; if we are rejected, it is the Lord who is rejected. We are the channels of the message, not its source.

Each one of us as Christians has authority to preach the gospel, and (if our faith stretches so far) to heal the sick and drive out demons. Whosoever's sins we forgive, they are forgiven; whosoever's sins we do not forgive, they remain (Jn.20.23). What vast authority! But here is the strength of that authority: we possess none of it personally. It is simply a declaratory authority. The sacrifice of the cross alone causes sins to be forgiven, and when someone becomes a disciple of Jesus and draws near, as it were, to the foot of the cross, we can say, 'Today salvation has come to this house.' The new convert can be reassured that they have a relationship with the Father. But the salvation and the forgiveness are not at our discretion, any more than our proclamation that 'Christ is risen' makes the resurrection true or untrue. Our authority is the word of God; we can say that 'this person's sins are forgiven', not because we have made any decision on the matter, but because we have inside information about the basis upon which forgiveness of sins is available, and in the case of a person who repents and has become a follower of Jesus, we know that the basis applies. So we can assure the new disciple, 'your sins are forgiven'. The same is true of 'our authority' in Christ generally: it is a declaration and (insofar as words have force in themselves) in that sense an enactment, of what Jesus has already done. Jesus tells Peter that 'Whatever you bind on earth will be bound in heaven, and whatever you loose on earth will be loosed in heaven' (Matt.16.19). But the form of the verbs employed (the future periphrastic passive!) means —even though it would make very ungainly English—

that 'whatever you bind on earth will be that which has already been bound in heaven'.

The point is this: the Message does not belong to us. On the contrary, we belong to it! We are not our own; we are bought with a price. The authority that we exercise does not inhere in us, for those who accept it are are accepting Someone else; those who reject it are rejecting Someone far greater. There is no need to defend 'my ministry', and so really to defend myself. There is no need to push or shove my way to the front. If my ministry is from God, he can do what he wants with it. If it is rejected by men, it is either because they are right, in which case I must repent, or because they do not wish to hear from God, in which case they will bear their judgement. Either way, there is no call for me to get worked up over it. When people revile us, and beat us, and persecute us, and say all manner of evil against us falsely on account of Jesus, he calls us to rejoice, because that's how they treated the prophets who came before us! A repudiation of our ministry? If anything, such suffering authenticates it.

The disciples, however, could not help taking a sly delight in their own exercise of authority. There is a certain smugness, not far below the surface, in their observation (v.17) that 'even the demons submit to us in your name'. (The 'in your name' seems to be the spiritual 'saving clause' that makes it all right to gloat over the fact that the demons 'submit to *us*'.) So Jesus ignores it and goes on to talk about Satan falling like lightning from heaven. The apparent disconnectedness of this piece of dialogue is noteworthy. Such abrupt changes abound in John's gospel, but that is probably because of editorial considerations on John's part; in the context of Luke, they are rarer, and so this instance is likely to be significant. Jesus pointedly chooses not to pick up on the disciples' comment, initially at least. They are excited, but he is not. They are ecstatic that some few local demons have submitted, but Jesus sees the cosmic picture, and the fate of Satan himself. We likewise often miss the big picture because we are taken up with small, self-validating details.

Jesus then reminds the disciples of the authority that they do have, but adds a pointed 'However'. There is no room for boasting of their own authority (for in truth it is not their own at all), whether over demons or over anything else. If they wish to rejoice—and they should— let it be because their names are written in heaven. 'Do not celebrate your supposed power and authority', says Jesus 'but rejoice over your dependence.' Whether or not a demon submits to me 'in Jesus' name' is a matter full of consequences for the demon, and the person whom he is oppressing. But for me, whilst it may provide some temporary excitement, the whole affair is at least relatively trivial. I know that there will be some who will remind Jesus on the last day that they drove out demons in his name, and did other things besides, and yet will hear him say, 'I never knew you. Away from me, you evildoers!' (Matt.7.22–23). No. The weightiest matter of all for me is whether my name is written in heaven. I cannot 'exercise authority' over that, or use a 'power ministry' to bring it about. For that I am dependent, obviously and utterly. Not only does the fact that I drive out demons not save me, but it is not even evidence, on its own at least, that I am amongst the redeemed.

So a ministry of power is fine, indeed it is very good, as long as we realize that it is Jesus' power and his alone, and that none of the authority belongs to us. But as we exercise it, there will be a constant temptation to fasten onto the delusion that it does belong to us, and so Jesus warns us not to develop a fixation with 'authority', or indeed with supernatural phenomena at all. If there is something to rejoice in, it can only ever be that our names are written in heaven.

In the light of all this, the marked tendency of so many of us to speak about 'taking authority' over situations is rather jarring. It is not, usually, that the aspirations are wrong. 'We take authority in the name of Jesus over the spirit of oppression in Martin's life' is superspiritual psychobabble, but it expresses a perfectly godly aim, namely to see Martin free, either in his outward circumstances or in his mental state, from things that are entangling him and holding him back from following Christ. So why can't we pray that? To use the authority rhetoric gives us delusions about ourselves and our true place. It also turns the one doing the praying (presumably over Martin's bowed head!) into some kind of a priest. Indeed, the idea of seeing certain Christians as priests—mediators between God and man—in respect of their fellow believers is not at all far-fetched if we think of the adulation given to those with 'power ministries' by at least some of their followers. One could point also to the various attempts to identify the precise origins of the 'Toronto blessing' in some one particular meeting or prophecy, and to trace its progress from there—as if for all the world we were seeking some kind of apostolic succession.

Power and authority inhere in Jesus, not in us. Jesus himself tells us as much. 'All authority in heaven and on earth has been given to me. Therefore go and make disciples of all nations . . .' (Matt.28.18–19). The fact that all authority rests with Jesus is itself the guarantee and the condition for our own ministry. As we fulfil Jesus' commission, we will do many wonderful things 'in the name of Jesus', and when we do we will be tempted to slip into thinking that authority rests in us. The distinction is a fine one, but it is one we neglect at our peril.

PART III

Equipping the Saints

It has to be said, however, that the structures of our church life don't always lend themselves to making full use of everybody's gifting. To begin with, most of our meetings are dominated by what some have called 'a single voice'. A leader stands at the front and directs the worship, then gives out the notices, then leads in prayer, and then proceeds to preach. Of course, often these tasks are divided up, though usually not between more than two or three people. The differences between denominations are usually quite slight in this respect (except, perhaps, for the Brethren). Anglicans, strongly Reformed churches, middle-of-the-road Baptists, even Pentecostals and house churches: the meetings of all of them tend to be dominated by the contributions of, at most, a handful of people. The two last-mentioned categories of church have not always been like this, and some are still very open in terms of participation, but most have become more formalized.

In the early church, both in the New Testament period itself (one thinks of 1 Cor.14) and afterwards, there is evidence that many people spoke in Christian worship meetings. Services only gradually became more formal and, once Christianity became a way of controlling society, after the fourth century, such informality as having a wide range of people taking part in services ceased altogether. Still, the Anabaptists of the sixteenth-century frequently had many active participants in services, and the English General Baptists of the seventeenth century also put a low priority on worship being led from the front. One outraged person complained about the Baptists who met in Thomas Lambe's church in Bell Alley, Coleman Street in London that several preachers would speak in succession and 'when one hath done, there's sometimes difference in the church who shall exercise next, 'tis put to the vote, some for one, some for another'. Furthermore, it was 'usual and lawful, not only for the company to stand up and object against the doctrine delivered when the exerciser of his gifts hath made an end, but in the midst of it'.[1] Perhaps the Baptists' practice was bordering on the disorderly, notwithstanding the fact that they were in a revival situation; even so, their critic, the Presbyterian Thomas Edwards, was not exactly impartial.

What is certain is that vigorous, growing, radical churches will tend to make space for a wide variety of people. Their congregations will not be content to sit passively whilst they are lectured by one all-wise patriarch at the front. After a recent sermon, one lady was kind enough to express appreciation to me during the coffee-and-milling-about-time afterwards, but then raised a query about something I'd said. We discussed the point in question for a couple of minutes and then she added, 'I wish I could have stuck my hand up at the time, and said "Excuse me, what about . . .?" ' It occurred to me to counter with, 'Why didn't you, then?' but I was not so cruel. We both knew the answer to that. In contrast to the situation in the early church, and radical groups in history, such a thing is just 'not done' in our churches. Instead, we are playing at Puritans: one person gives a talk in authoritative fashion, whilst the rest of us sit there appreciatively and take notes. That is how the Puritan preachers of the late sixteenth and seventeenth centuries behaved and, in their minds' eyes, it is these people whom most of our preachers, whether full-time pastors or lay people, are attempting to emulate. But Puritanism was about patriarchy; it was unavoidably tied up with a vision of Christianity as a means of social control. And most of our preaching is about a patriarchal figure telling a submissive group of people what is good for them. No wonder some leaders are less than pleased to find someone with a theological education in their congregation. There are plenty of

[1] Cited in M.Tolmie, *The Triumph of the Saints* (Cambridge Univ. Press, 1977), pp.76–77. See also Alan Kreider, 'Worship and Evangelism in Pre-Christendom', *Vox Evangelica* (1994), pp.25–26; Eleanor Kreider, 'A Vision of Multi-Voiced Worship', *Anabaptism Today* (Issue 5, February, 1994), pp.13–17.

'good spiritual reasons' that can be deployed to discourage any of the flock from getting such an education,
unless the person concerned plans to become a pastor, in
which case they will leave their present congregation to
lead another one and so cannot be a 'threat'.

Such a system encourages 'star' preachers who are
strong on rhetoric and able to hold the rest of us in awe
of their skills. So ministry comes to mean domination,
encouraging would-be leaders in the audience to adopt
the same pattern of behaviour, while the others assume
they have nothing (even questions) to contribute. Would
an occasional time of questions, gently and lovingly
conducted on all sides, really undermine 'the authority'
of the preacher? (As if that is what mattered!) Might it
not help us to move forward together, and give us a
collective opportunity to 'own' what has just been said?
Wouldn't it help us to really learn from the teaching in
church? This is not theory: I have seen it in practice, and
even been on the receiving end of the questions. The
sense of collective advance that a congregation experiences from such a procedure is tremendous. And it also
helps the preacher to remember his place.

We noticed a moment ago that some churches had
become more formalized, that is, dominated by a few
voices, only in more recent times. And here we come to
a crucial point. It is a constant of church history that
new, lively, growing movements in the church have a
habit of getting everybody involved. They tend to have
plural leadership and very little hierarchy. In real re-
vivals, every-member ministry is the norm. Only when a
movement starts to stagnate does the amount of structure increase, both in terms of the conduct of meetings
and in church government. Eventually, the movement
gravitates back to one-man leadership, and the church is
once more dependent upon some great leader preaching
up a storm to bring about revival. It is interesting that
the early church did not grow in this fashion. To be sure,
Paul and his teams spoke to the groups of uncircum-
cised Gentiles who attended the synagogues as 'second-

rate' Jews, and these responded quickly for obvious reasons: they already knew who God was, what the moral law was, what sin was—in a word, they needed only the good news of a Saviour. But for two and a half centuries thereafter the church grew through the witness and ministry of all its members; pagans knew nothing of God, and most needed to be taught the basics over years. Open evangelism was out of the question because of persecution. There were no 'superstars', unless one counts martyrs like Polycarp in Asia, or the slave-girl Blandina in Lyons, or the young mother Perpetua, her friend Saturus and her slave Felicitas in North Africa. But growth was dramatic.

Renewal and revival are accompanied by every-member participation, partly because renewal and revival naturally produce great enthusiasm amongst ordinary Christians, but partly because renewal and growth require everybody to be involved. God can do what he wants, and he can act without us. But in general he chooses to act through his people. This is part of the vast dynamism—and the appeal—of Pentecostalism in the Third World: every member takes part.

It is this every-member aspect which the charismata are all about. You don't need to be educated or eloquent, or a great leader, to give a word in tongues, or a prophecy; you just need to be hearing from God. That is why, with the growing institutionalization of the early church, they began to die out. Justin Martyr, a Christian leader in the mid-second century, noted the use of the gifts, mentioning especially prophecy. Irenæus, a church leader in Gaul (modern France) around the year 200, spoke of the gifts of the Spirit which Paul had described in 1 Corinthians as being frequently active in his own day. But even in the second century they were being used less than before, and the schismatic Montanist movement was partly concerned to correct this decline. Origen, a teacher in Egypt in the early third century, spoke of the gifts as still operative, but his repeated use of the words 'still' and 'traces' shows that they were

beginning to die out. It is no accident that this process
was parallel with the growing emphasis on hierarchy,
formal services with an ever larger place given to liturgy, and services led by one man at the front, increasingly called 'the bishop'. (Paul had always referred to
'elders' in the plural for each church.) Finally, once
Christianity had become the official religion of the late
Roman Empire, Augustine wrote that tongues had been
a gift meant only for the time of the apostles. As a
historical statement, this was clearly wrong, but if Christianity is about keeping people in order, one cannot
afford to have people hearing from God and sharing the
fact in services, as this would disrupt things! So the gifts
of the Spirit had to go.

This was an extreme position, but a milder version of
the same thing tends to happen in many groups, as
formal leadership structures and standardized proce-
dures take over. During the early years of the Quakers,
in the seventeenth century, prophesying was practised,
and there were numerous healings. George Fox, one of
the most important early leaders, even wrote a book
describing them all. But Fox lived to be an old man, and
by the time of his death the movement was already
beginning to fossilize. The Society of Friends wouldn't
even publish the book, because they were by then
embarrassed by his claims, and forbade members to
prophesy.

At the birth of Methodism in the eighteenth century,
people danced for joy in the meetings, some fell down
under conviction of sin, and women preached. The
Welsh Methodists were described by their enemies as
'Welsh jumpers'! But, with the later institutionalization
of the churches born in the Great Awakening, all of that
early excitement and participation died away. Similarly,
there was speaking in tongues at Edward Irving's
church in London in the 1830s but, after the death of the
early leaders of the movement he founded, prophecy
and tongues were no longer used, and by 1868 J.B.
Cardale, an influential leader, had published a book to

show that prophecy was no longer needed! On anec-
dotal evidence, I would venture a guess that many
modern Pentecostal and house churches, in Britain at
least, use the gifts of the Spirit less now than they did in
their earlier phases.

And always the pattern is the same. As movement
grows into machine, and finally into monument, liturgy
squeezes out life, structure squeezes out substance,
anointing succumbs to administration, and gifting to
good order. Where things have gone right and there has
been vibrant spiritual life, it is possible to make a clear
connection between renewal and revival on the one
hand, and plural leadership, every-member (including
women's) ministry and the use of spiritual gifts on the
other.

The gifts of the Spirit have always acted as the great
equalizer. They guarantee that you, too, whoever you
are, if you are a Christian, can share and bring something to your brothers and sisters. 'When you come
together, everyone has a hymn, or a word of instruction,
a revelation, a tongue or an interpretation' (1 Cor.14.26).
We all have something that we can contribute.

When Paul was giving instruction to the church in
Corinth about the use of spiritual gifts, he gave the
examples of supernaturally provided wisdom and
knowledge, 'faith' (presumably for some specific situation), gifts of healing, miracles, prophecy, a supernatural
ability to discern divine spiritual activity from the de-
monic, and the abilities to speak in tongues and to
interpret them (1 Cor.12.8–10). With sadly predictable
legalism, a number of Christians have leapt to the
conclusion that there are therefore precisely nine spiritual gifts, and that these alone are to be recognized by
the church and sought by the Christian. As always, they
end up merely imprisoning themselves inside the box
into which they had attempted to insert God. A friend of
mine once worked for a Christian organization which
insisted that any gifts not on these lists were 'only
natural'! Paul himself, however, later in the very same

chapter (v.28), mentions a variety of other giftings—
apostles, prophets, teachers, abilities in helping others
and gifts of administration—as well as repeating himself
concerning some of those he had mentioned before. In
his letter to the Romans, he gives a different, and again
only partially overlapping, list of charismata (Rom.12.6–
8). The implied open-endedness is unavoidable; Paul
had neither the intention nor the desire to give a defini-
tive list of gifts and ministries. That is because he was
happy to leave more to the imagination and initiative of
individual Christians and churches than many modern
leaders are willing to leave to theirs. You can insist that
a producer of Christian computer software comes under
'gifts of administration', and shoehorn Christian rock-
bands into the category of 'evangelists' if you wish, but
the obvious fact is that many ministries are possible only
under the conditions of the given society and techno-
logical environment in which they operate. And if ministries can be specific to particular cultures, they can also
be so to specific individuals. One sometimes hears the
affirmation that 'God respects our individuality', but
this understatement betrays a misunderstanding of the
situation: he created our individuality in the first place!
It is precisely through our individuality that God
chooses to work. The gifts and ministries he gives will
be as diverse as the people who exercise them. They will
not fit into a series of neat little pigeon-holes based on
some Christian group's understanding of one or other of
the lists given in the Pauline epistles.

If we do not believe that Jesus' unique work in us is of
any value, we will attempt to substitute something else
for it in order to be acceptable in the eyes of our
Christian brothers and sisters. Our family discovered
this when, over a period of about six years, we had to
move house several times. Each time, we joined a
slightly different type of church from the one we had
been used to before moving. Each church was perfectly
(or at least, averagely) spiritual, and so, I think, were we,
but the spirituality in each new church was expressed in

a different way from that in our old one. The favoured
jargon phrases, the most popular choruses and the kind
of attitudes they encouraged, the tone of the preaching,
and the nuances of the way people talked and acted
were . . . well, just a little different. At first, we continued
'being spiritual' in the way that our old church had
moulded us into 'being spiritual', and whilst this didn't
mean we were unacceptable in the new environment,
our new companions would tend to treat us with a
mixture of faint suspicion and patronizing indulgence
for a probationary period. Within a few months we
would acclimatize to the new emotional temperature
and the new jargon. And with this change, our status
within the community would adjust to one of full
acceptance as 'OK people'. What had happened? We
had been judged by our initial failure to conform to, and
then later by our compliance with, a set of group
norms—turns of phrase, smiling in the right places and
all the other social trivia—which were accepted as indic-
ative of being a healthy, spiritual Christian in that
particular environment. We had also, of course, yielded
to peer-group pressure. Most people who move home
face the same experience; it's one of the many things
that makes 'finding a new church' such a trial.

But what all parties involved are doing, both newcomers and the receiving community alike, is assuming
that true Christian spirituality has to express itself in a
uniform way. We are all familiar with the shibboleths
that have obtained in various evangelical circles at different times about alcohol and tobacco. But one church
we belonged to briefly on our travels had an extraordinarily high proportion of families with four or more
children, and I'm certain it was no accident. Nothing
was ever said, and it didn't need to be, but if you
wanted to be like the really godly people in the church,
then you knew what to do. My wife and I had our hands
full with three children, so this was one church where
we resigned ourselves to a life on the margins!

Now, at the level of the cultural trivia which define how one Christian group or congregation chooses to express itself, perhaps this doesn't matter too much. But the problem becomes much more serious when we try to copy individual forceful personalities. God wants to deal with each one of us in a unique way. The trouble is, most of us tend to look at some other Christian whom we really respect, and attempt to reproduce that other person's spiritual experience and the characteristics of their ministry. So we try to talk like them and act like them. At its best, this is merely embarrassingly stupid. At its worst, one or other of two results must necessarily follow. Either we will fail to be like our hero-figure, in which case we will feel unanointed, and see ourselves as someone who, really, has let God down. Even more disastrously, we may end up with a false religiosity by convincing others—and even ourselves—that we have succeeded. At that point, the distinctive features of the hero-figure become absolutized: truly spiritual people do such-and-such, or buy such-and-such; people really moving in the Spirit never do so-and-so. An American friend once told me of a church he began visiting years ago in one of the southern states: the preacher had an emotional style and, towards the end of each sermon, would begin to plead with his congregation to accept the spiritual truth he was presenting to them, pulling out a handkerchief and dabbing away his tears as he did so. Impressed by the compassion God seemed to have given the preacher for his congregation, my friend visited nearby churches of the same denomination. He found that the preachers there did exactly the same thing. It was just the way of being 'truly spiritual' within that subculture; God had little to do with it.

Where did the special 'prayer voice' come from—the sanctimonious tone that tells all who hear it that the one praying is truly fervent? In South Wales, the word 'God' in public prayers is often pronounced with six 'G's and nine 'd's. Why? Someone said it that way once and a lot of other someones felt it sounded really impressive. So in certain circles it's been the done thing ever since. For similar reasons, prophecies in meetings tend to be uttered at full shriek in long, convoluted sentences. There are several different preaching styles, but few of them are much of an approximation to natural speech, and most of them are conscious or unconscious imitations of the preachers' own heroes.

Why do we act like this? Mostly, it is because we do not have sufficient confidence in the value and legitimacy of God's distinctive and unique work in us. I feel inadequate because my present spiritual experience doesn't measure up to what I think yours is, or what seems to be the experience of the author of the latest devotional paperback I've read. But my perceptions of both (especially the latter!) are likely to be mistaken. Even if they are not, I do not need to attempt to be somebody else. God wants to deal with me in a unique way, for true anointing is when God takes hold of *me*, with my own personality, warts and all, to use for his glory. The apostle Paul was short, seems to have been unappealing to look at, and complained to the end that his speech was contemptible. Peter was over-hasty, and talked too much. But God was with them. Neither needed to become someone else; an open channel was enough.

Your uniqueness and mine, and that of our fellow-Christians, ensures an immense variety of charismata, 'according to the measure of Christ's gift'. We don't need to spend our lives attempting to be carbon copies of someone else, and then flagellating ourselves because we aren't and can't be. What matters is what God is doing within us to conform us to the image of Christ. If we are Christian leaders, we should not be seeking to turn out followers in our own image, but to seek the development of each unique individual.

EIGHT

Enablers ... or Corks?

> It was he who gave some to be apostles, some to be
> prophets, some to be evangelists, and some to be pastors
> and teachers, to prepare God's people for works of
> service, so that the body of Christ may be built up
> (Eph.4.11–12).

In the last chapter, we noticed that new movements tend
to become more institutionalized over a period of time,
and that every-member ministry gives way to the leadership, and eventually the priesthood, of a few leaders.
The clergy-laity split re-emerges. What is happening
when this takes place is that we Christians are allowing
leaders to 'be the church' on behalf of the rest of us. This
way of thinking is illustrated quite clearly in the old-
fashioned phrase used to describe someone becoming a
clergyman: 'he's gone into the church'. The implication
is quite clear: before he became a cleric he was not 'in
the church', and now he is; only clergy are 'in the
church'; the rest of us simply attend. The expression
'going to church' reflects the same mentality. (Christians
are the church, for goodness' sake!) When we allow
someone to 'be the church' on our behalf, we effectively
extricate ourselves from responsibility and involvement;

we become, quite literally, 'hearers of the word' rather than 'doers'.

The process whereby the thrust of activity passes from being the concern of everyone in the church to being the preserve of a few leaders is the exact reverse of the pattern which Paul sets out in Ephesians. The very purpose of ministries such as apostles, prophets and the others being given was so that 'God's people' would be prepared 'for works of service'. Leaders would equip others, so that they could do the work instead. That is the point of Paul's instruction to Timothy: 'the things you have heard me say in the presence of many witnesses entrust to reliable men who will also be qualified to teach others' (2 Tim.2.2). Even restricted to its literal meaning, Paul's sentence envisages at least four links in the chain: Paul, Timothy, 'reliable men', 'others'. As we have seen when looking at different types of ministry, an unnecessarily literal interpretation of this kind of practical instruction (just four stages) is perhaps the least helpful way to use Paul's letters; he meant that the message and the ministry were to be passed on, and on, and on, without limit! The pattern of gifting, anointing and being equipped to serve Jesus in the church and the world was away from the few and towards the many; the apostles prepared God's people to serve in building up the body of Christ. So rarely has the movement been in this direction, however, that, on the few occasions it really has, it might almost be accorded the status of miracle.

Leadership is about equipping others. This seems so obvious and uncontentious that mentioning it might be thought almost unnecessary, but the fact is that most leadership as it is actually practised in churches and Christian organizations is really geared towards fostering dependency. The great preacher preaches and builds up a circle of devotees; their lives may not change, but they like listening to him as people might enjoy watching *Star Trek*. It is a characteristic of cults, of course, that leaders bind followers to themselves and their teachings

until they are unable to make the smallest move without
reference to those leaders. Christians abhor the cults, but
their leadership style can often amount to a milder
version of the same thing. Real Christian leadership,
however, is about doing the opposite of this; it does not
create dependency but, on the contrary, it equips those
who are receiving the ministry and leaves them spiritually stronger and more confident of their own situation in Christ and in their ability to act for him than they
were before.

Perhaps we should not simply blame leaders for
encouraging the dependency mindset. Often enough,
non-leaders seem only too willing to slip into it of their
own accord. Paul himself had cause to scold the Corinthians for giving exactly this kind of adulation; indeed, he was even the unhappy recipient of some of it.
'One of you says, "I follow Paul"; another, "I follow
Apollos"; another, "I follow Cephas"; still another, "I
follow Christ." ' (1 Cor.1.12) Personally, I find it consoling that some of the Corinthian Christians answered
their fellows with 'I follow Christ'; even then there were
superspirituals who felt that, by coming out with an
unanswerable pious platitude, they had somehow risen
above a serious problem or answered a hard question!
Paul was concerned about the divisions this situation
caused, but its roots were in the tendency to elevate
leaders to a point where they are somehow set apart
from other Christians, and this is what Paul roundly
condemns: 'Was Paul crucified for you? Were you bap-
tised into the name of Paul? ... What, after all, is
Apollos? And what is Paul? Only servants, through
whom you came to believe—as the Lord has assigned to
each his task. I planted the seed, Apollos watered it, but
God made it grow. So neither he who plants nor he who
waters is anything, but only God who makes things
grow' (1 Cor.1.13; 3.5–7).

'Neither he who plants nor he who waters is
anything'—how many leaders really believe this, and
act in a way that encourages their flocks to believe it

too? If we really refuse to cultivate dependency in those whom we are discipling, if we are really eager only to equip others, then one consequence is sure to follow. Those whom we have taught, or led, or ministered to, will not need us any more. Indeed, the fact that 'our' lambs have come to such a point will be, in a sense, a measure of success. Our teaching and directing will tend to throw our hearers back onto the resources of God, rather than eagerly anticipating the next sermon or session with us. We will encourage them to experiment with the first steps in fields of service that are appropriate to them at the time, and as they do so allow them to relax in the certain knowledge that they are free to make mistakes without ridicule or condemnation. We will direct them to books and other resources they can consult for themselves. We will direct them to others who can help in specific areas (and, as they grow, we will subtly—or lovingly—direct others to them, so that they can experience the growth and increased confidence that inevitably results from being a source of help, rather than its object). Always, the focus will be upon God and his work in their own hearts, with our own leadership acting simply as a supportive framework.

Some years ago, I led a group of young people for worship, Bible study, evangelism, and many other things. They used to come and ask me all kinds of questions, earnestly wanting to know my opinion. Of course, they do not do this any longer. I am still in touch with many of them, but they certainly do not weigh my opinion on anything we discuss more heavily than those of any of their other friends. Or than their own. They have grown up, not only as people but as Christians, and as a result they do not need me any more. Most of them are actively engaged in ministries of their own, leading house-groups, worship, involved in evangelism. It's very rewarding to know that, for at least a part of their journey into Christian and personal maturity, I had some input. One of the group grew up, got married and moved away from the area so that I'd pretty much lost contact with her, although I knew she was continuing as a strong and mature Christian. But a while ago a perfect stranger came up and introduced herself to me and then said, 'I'm Emma's best friend. She always remembers you with fondness.' It was a wonderful, but humbling, moment. Another member of the group now leads a congregation belonging to one of the house-church networks—something I doubt I would ever be able to do—and probably doesn't think of me from one year to the next. But I think of him. And it's a good feeling.

Sadly, there were one or two who fell by the wayside. If it were possible to re-establish a friendship or relationship with one of them again, they would need to have the basics of Christian faith reinstalled in their lives. They are the ones who would have to allow themselves to be guided, and simply to listen to what I had to tell them. And that dependency would be a sign of failure. It is the successes who have outgrown the need to be guided by me.

Something similar is true when we have children. As babies they have to learn the words we tell them, and what meanings to attach to those words. But the purpose is for them to learn enough so that they are able to express their own thoughts. By the time they are of school age, they have picked up enough nuances of language to be able to tell us jokes. Usually before they are teenagers, they have enough command of language and ideas to be able to argue with us! Eventually they leave and set up home on their own. Everything they have been taught will have served to make them more independent, and to have less need of their parents and teachers. Would we really want it any other way?

All of us involved in leadership need to be asking ourselves whether we are really equipping others, like old birds teaching young birds how to fly so that they will eventually soar away on their own, or whether we are actually fostering dependency and a fan-club for ourselves and our own wonderful brand of ministry. If the former, then we should be aiming to do ourselves out of a job; the people we are teaching will have learned to do for themselves what we have been showing them, and at least some of them will have grown to the point where they can take on the tasks that we have been doing, and perhaps do them better than we have. By that time, perhaps we will have grown ourselves so that it is time to do other tasks, or perhaps it will simply be the occasion to begin again with different people.

But how, it might be asked, can someone who is 'the minister' in some particular congregation possibly be expected to endorse the conclusions we have reached? To do so may entail the undermining of his position. If others are empowered to teach and to lead, then the pastor becomes, by degrees, powerless, and finally redundant. It is, I admit, a difficulty, but only if it is taken as axiomatic that the pastor is building his own career rather than the kingdom of Christ. To see the latter increase, it may be necessary for us to decrease. The alternative is to tell people week by week that we want them to grow in Christ but then deny them, especially the potential leaders among them, the scope to develop their gifts.

Seen in this light, all of the built-in frustrations of the bureaucratically appointed and bureaucratically functioning one-man leader are brought out in sharp relief. To encourage the potential worship leader to the point where she is actually able to lead worship is to renounce control of a major part of the service which, as 'the pastor', one might be expected to dominate. To include others in reading Scriptures, giving words of prophecy, sharing testimonies, giving exhortations, praying aloud etc. is to reduce one's own role to that of co-ordinator. And to hand over the precious pulpit to gifted lay-people—why, one's job has all but disappeared! Besides, the congregation are paying you; you at least have to be seen to be earning your salary!

In the same way, leaders often find that they themselves are not free to share in precisely that close personal fellowship of the body of the church to which they
exhort others. Supportive relationships mean vulner-
ability and, however good this may be for the sheep, the
shepherd knows that to reveal weaknesses, even acci-
dentally, to anyone inside the church is to give hostages
to fortune in the murderous fratricidal warfare that
passes under the description of 'church politics'. So
leaders and their spouses remain aloof, assuming a
benevolent and caring, and yet lofty and detached,
attitude with those entrusted to them. Mostly, they are
more akin to a type of spiritual GP than anything else.

If this sounds too harsh, I should at once add that
leaders can hardly be blamed for taking refuge from the
rest of us. We have a model of Christian leadership
which demands that the leader be respected, and those
at the helm are understandably afraid that, if we really
knew them as closely as all that, respect is the last thing
they would get. So they take refuge in distance and a
bureaucratic model of authority, in which the leader is
the omnicompetent paid professional. But the omni-
competence of the leader demands that no one else
become too competent. And that in turn means that the
saints be entertained and overawed rather than
equipped.

How would it be if we turned all of this on its head?
How if we were prepared to pay the price of being
known, and hence genuinely vulnerable, to those whom
we seek to lead? How if we were so impassioned to feed
Jesus' lambs, and to 'present everyone perfect in Christ',
that we were prepared to take whatever were the consequences of doing so, even if that meant being replaced
by someone whom we ourselves had encouraged or
equipped? What would the consequences matter com-
pared to the gains? Whose kingdom are we building
anyway? Where does our security truly lie? The harvest
remains plentiful; it is only the workers who are few, so

there will always be more work to do, even if the security of our present ministry is taken away.

Paul said concerning the teaching ministry of his own team of workers that 'We proclaim him, admonishing and teaching everyone with all wisdom, so that we may present everyone perfect [some translations say "mature"] in Christ' (Col.1.28). The 'so that' is important. The teaching and admonishing were not ends in themselves, but means to the real end, which was maturity in Christ for those who acted upon what they heard. And maturity, as with children becoming adults, means outgrowing dependence. Paul and his team exemplified this in their own ministries. They moved from place to place, making disciples, establishing them in the faith, building churches and then moving on. In Ephesus, Paul stayed for three years, but that seems to have been the longest it took him to make himself redundant.

What lesson are we supposed to learn from this? That we should all be constantly peripatetic, never tied to one place or group of people, and wandering around in some chaotic fashion? Obviously not. Paul's ministry is looked upon by almost all Christians as completely exceptional: he was involved in the earliest years of the church when the imperative was to spread the message as widely as possible as fast as possible. He was also a missionary, a calling which obviously requires some moving about. But that does not make the history of his ministry irrelevant to those of us with very different callings. Paul's mission was one of the most successful ever, and his ability to work himself so quickly out of a job was part of the measure of his success. The crucial lesson for all of us is his willingness to let go of the works he had built up, to stop controlling them, and allow them to take on a life of their own. Unless he did so, the entire purpose of the work would be frustrated. His teaching was done precisely in order to present people mature in Christ. He knew that the work of the apostle was to equip the saints to do the work of service so that *they*, not he, would continue the work of building up the body of Christ. The teaching he gave to Timothy was to be passed on by that young man to others, *not* so that they would become devotees of Timothy, but so that they in their turn could teach more people and see them equipped. The leader is to give himself or herself away.

The alternative is that we become 'corks in the bottle', afraid of seeing others develop for fear of undermining our own position. One church I know of experienced a wonderful period of growth, both spiritually and numerically, during the 1970s. The gifts of the Holy Spirit were poured out amongst the members of the congregation, worship was renewed, practical caring initiatives were undertaken in the neighbourhood, and many people living nearby were gloriously converted. The minister was happy to see this outpouring of blessing, but it soon became apparent that what was happening was bigger than he was. Over the years that followed, various leadership ministries began to blossom in the church: a youth leader grew into an extaordinarily gifted evangelist, a house-group leader emerged as a brilliant pastor, a young person with exceptional teaching gifts would be introduced from the outside by the denomination. But one by one, they all left, and the congregation was thus deprived of these expressions of its growth and best human resources for its future growth. The reason? The minister felt threatened by those who were clearly more gifted than he was, and found all manner of ways of restricting their activities, and 'good' reasons for doing so. The members of the congregation became utterly despondent once the pattern of events had become plain, and when it had become obvious that the minister would allow nothing to happen that he did not have the ability to control. The once lively congregation began to stagnate, and continued to decline until his retirement a few years ago. Regretfully, it seems that the security of his position was more precious than the equipping of the saints.

Another device employed by insecure or authoritarian leaders is to promote people of inappropriate abilities to the ranks immediately underneath themselves. People whose gifts are emphatically not in the area of leadership are pushed forward, of course, because they are no possible threat to the leader who promoted them. Where this happens—and it occurs all too frequently—it generally leads to long-term disaster; the leader has secured his own immediate future at the cost of the future of the flock for whom he is ostensibly caring. When the original leader eventually passes from the scene, the second-rank people have to take over as the new first rank, and the church ends up being led by non-leaders. These are usually secretly aware of the fact, and so even more insecure in their own position, and inclined to rely on bureaucratic models of authority as a way of protecting themselves. Churches or Christian organizations in this position tend to lose all sense of vision and to become totally directionless. It is not an infallible rule, but one can often assess the true heart of a leader by the people to whom he or she has devolved responsibilities.

These painful issues are emphatically not the concern only of those who write 'minister' on forms asking for their occupation; all of us involved in leadership have to confront them. One of the real difficulties is that few of us are consciously manipulative, and almost all of us would be horrified at the thought that we are aiming to control or dominate others. Yet it is observably true that manipulation, control and domination are the drift of many of our actions, and the net result in very many Christian circles. If we're not acting from malice, why is this so?

Part of the problem is that we all need to be needed. I want people to like me, and the more important I am to them, the happier I am. This is inevitable, and not really wrong, but it is also a possible source of danger and abuse when this factor drives my relationship with others, particularly with those I am leading in a Christian context. The fact is, if my wish to be indispensable to others is fulfilled, that has the direct effect of making those others dependent upon me. My indispensability and their dependence are different sides of the same coin. The former may be a sort of half-admitted goal, but the latter, to which I would never admit, is part of the inevitable result.

Another factor that needs to be borne in mind is that a number of Christians positively *want* to be led by a decisive, dominating leader, and are easily convinced that this is somehow the will of God. They like authoritarian Christian leaders for reasons similar to those which cause others to like authoritarian political leaders: 'at least they're decisive'; 'they know where they're going'; 'I respect their authority'. If one thinks like this, one need not carry burdens about the state of the church, worry lest evangelism is being stressed too little, or something else too much. The leaders know; they have a plan, and everything will sort itself out! This is, of course, an abdication of responsibility. If leaders know best, one does not need to choose, to think, or even, in some contexts, to participate in more than a perfunctory way. We can simply let the leaders 'be the church' on behalf of the rest of us.

For whatever reasons, the 'controlling' urge tends to take on a momentum of its own and, in one way or another, too many of us who are leaders stumble into patterns of behaviour which perpetuate the infancy of those we claim to serve. Will we be enablers and equippers of others? Or will we be corks in the bottle, intent upon guarding and buttressing our own positions? We all like control, and we're all very good at thinking of perfectly spiritual reasons why we should have more of it in the context where we happen to be serving. But if we are really *serving*, then we will be willing to let go, and to 'do nothing out of selfish ambition or vain conceit' (Phil.1.3), but in humility to consider others better than ourselves. It is certainly not something that comes easily to any of us. But at least we can recognize that this is something Jesus calls us to do.

NINE

Unity, Diversity and Body-Building

> Christ, from whom the whole body, being fitted and held together by that which every joint supplies, according to the proper working of each individual part, causes the growth of the body for the building up of itself in love (Eph.4.16, NASB).

If you are a leader, people will criticize you. There are two reasons for this. Firstly, they are human beings, and secondly, you deserve it. Like everyone else, leaders find it easier to concede the second point in general terms rather than in the specific. (Have you ever noticed how the only named failing most people are willing to own up to is impatience? 'I don't suffer fools gladly!') Even so, the first point is not without its problems, either. Of course, there is nothing more debilitating to Christian activities than constant whingeing; just as you are trying to get something going, somebody begins to complain about this or that, tells their friends and alienates them from whatever is happening, arguments start, and in the end no one even feels spiritual enough, let alone united enough, to proceed. It is very tempting to start using the pulpit to preach all those warnings about the 'divisive man' (Tit.3.10), and against 'quarrelling about words'

(2 Tim.2.14), or to point out that dissensions and factions are listed by Paul in Galatians alongside the sins of sexual immorality and witchcraft.

So it is not only authoritarian leaders who emphasize the need for 'unity' and 'positive thinking' in churches. Warring factions, negativity and backbiting are obviously harmful in any group of Christians. They do untold spiritual damage to the lives and the hearts of those who indulge in them, and they undermine the bonds of love that should draw us together. But leaders are more likely than other Christians to be anxious about such problems. After all, factions are either competing for the endorsement of leaders, in which case satisfying one will alienate the others, or are trying to replace the existing leadership altogether. In any case, the usual target for negativity and criticism *is* leaders, either explicitly and personally, or by implication, as when current practices and emphases of the church or group are criticized by some of its members. Any leader could live without this kind of trouble, and so the temptation to stifle every manifestation of discontent— or even of diversity and creativity—is strong, especially since such a formidable battery of Bible verses can be deployed to silence those whose ideas diverge from those of the leadership.

Not all dissent, or even criticism, in Christian groups is motivated by negativity or personal ambition, however. Far from it. The number of doctrinal and practical variations that are possible in expressing Christianity, even within the framework of a strict orthodoxy, is very great. Unless the leaders wish to indulge in a sort of theological 'ethnic cleansing' by purging their own groups of all who disagree with them, then they are going to have to live with at least some degree of pluralism, however strongly they will obviously wish to promote their own views and their own practical approaches to problems. Constantly, the leader needs to be asking, in such possible situations of conflict, 'What am I really seeking to uphold here—a spiritual principle of genuine importance for the life of the body? Or my own programme and my own authority?' Taken very far, indeed, the urge to foster unity and positive thinking can be simply another route to authoritarianism, and another weapon in the authoritarian's armoury once that situation has been reached. It is easy to stigmatize any and all criticism in order to bolster one's own position. Indeed, this is a classic tactic of the cults in battering their new recruits into submission, but the practice does not become harmless simply because the organization doing the battering is theologically orthodox.

Without creative dissent, none of the modern denominations would have come into being. The house-church people would still have been in the Brethren or Pentecostal churches, the Pentecostals would still be Methodists, the Brethren and the Methodists would have remained within the Church of England, the Baptists would have stayed with their separatist-Congregationalist roots, and these would in turn have stuck with the Anglicans . . . who would in *their* turn still be part of the Roman Catholic church! Indeed, Rome is where we would all be. By breaking away from the previous body, the founding fathers of each other group have committed precisely the kind of 'rebellion' that many of their successor-leaders now assure their own flocks is 'as the sin of witchcraft' (1 Sam.15.23 AV)!

Of course, almost all churches and Christian organizations are plagued by moaners and groaners, and people who genuinely do have a 'critical spirit', in the sense that they criticize for its own sake. These certainly need reproof, both for their own wellbeing and for the wellbeing of others who may take them seriously enough to be contaminated with the same hardness of heart. But 'critical spirit' is a dangerous expression, because it can be used by those with authoritarian instincts to stigmatize (by implication, to demonize) people who are not trying to be negative and destructive for its own sake, but who simply have something different to say. Often, superspiritual condemnations are used to marginalize gifted people of independent ideas who may be a threat to existing leaders. Where this happens, the problems of the disaffected are merely compounded, and no real unity is achieved except the sham of resentful submission to a dominant figure or figures.

Of course, the 'unity' and 'no criticism' rhetoric can be used to stifle and marginalize people with independent thinking, or those whose gifts are perceived as a possible threat. But those who have been excluded from influence in this way will feel frustrated. If they are sensitive, they will probably also end up feeling guilty. Peer-group pressure is a powerful force, as anyone who has had dealings with older children and teenagers knows. 'Perhaps it's just my pride. How can I be so sure that I'm in the right, when the official line of my church says something different?'

Tim is an example of just such a person. He was an extremely good worship leader. When he moved job and house, the new church was fairly welcoming of him, but not of his gifts. At first, of course, he could hardly expect to contribute. He was new, and the people in church needed to be satisfied that he was a solid, stable Christian before he could be included in such an important activity. In any case, Tim wasn't the sort of person who arrived amongst a new group of people and started bragging about his abilities. Even so, as people got to know him, and visited his flat, they could hardly help noticing the good quality piano, guitar and amplifier amongst his otherwise very modest possessions, as well as the stack of worship music on his shelves. He did lead worship, in a very small way, one evening when a house group met in his living room. Four months on, he mentioned to the elder who led worship that he was willing to help with the small music group in the church, but he still wasn't even invited to the practices on a Thursday night. All of this might have been tolerable if the worship leading in the congregation was good. But the fact was, it was chronic, as most of the members were well aware. The music was badly and insensitively played, and both slow and fast tunes were homogenized into a medium-paced beat. As a result, the worship in church was something of a non-event, and could hardly be described as uplifting. Tim wouldn't have dared to complain about this aspect of the church's life to anybody, in case it looked as though he was blowing his own trumpet, or playing church power games. As a result, he became the victim of those power games himself. A garbled report came back to him, *via* a friend, that the elder in question was unsure about the style of worship which Tim might introduce into the church, but in fact Tim was no revolutionary, and was simply longing to introduce a vastly better version of what was already happening. Tim strongly suspected that the elder's uncertainty was more claimed than genuine, and that his real fear was that Tim would make a success of leading worship, rather than the reverse. As the months went by Tim started to feel angry about the situation, but he was a sensitive soul, and his feelings alternated with guilt on account of the anger. He also worried that he was simply being proud, and that made him feel guilty too. Sometimes he got angry about the fact that he was being made to feel guilty ... and then he felt guilty about that.

Things don't have to be this way. Ralph, for example, is one of the 'biggest' men I know in church leadership. I do not mean that he is physically large, or even that he is particularly famous. He is simply assured of his own position in God, and well aware that the church belongs to Jesus and not to him. Although he is certainly intelligent, he is more working-class than most of the congregation he leads, yet he is never tempted to affectations or to inverted snobbery. Happy inside his own skin, he does not feel the need to defend himself, or to become aggressive in defence of his own very distinctive theological views. So when Phil, an articulate, educated newcomer with an established gift for preaching, moved into the area and into his congregation, Ralph had no qualms, after about three months of getting to know him, of offering him the pulpit one Sunday. Phil was surprised because, in one of their first long conversations, it had become apparent that their theological differences went all the way down to the ground in some areas, even though they were agreed on the essentials. 'Are you sure?' Phil queried. Ralph assured him that he was. Phil stressed that he would avoid 'abusing the pulpit' by dealing with anything contentious, but Ralph told him he should feel free to talk about whatever the Lord led him to say. Even so, Phil was as good as his word. The outcome was that his teaching helped a number of people and became a regular event. Everyone benefited. Phil's gifts did not go unused, and the church was encouraged. Doctrinal upheaval was avoided; indeed, some people were reminded that even Christians who held Phil's views were basically sound after all, and the whole affair became a matter of good-natured teasing on both sides. Even though it has worked out so well, Phil is still surprised that he was given such trust in the beginning. But as I said, Ralph is a big man.

For every person who is treated as Phil was, however, there are many more who suffer Tim's fate. Not only are the gifts and ideas of people like Tim denied to the church but, if they are kept unused and frustrated for long periods of time, the people involved are very likely to end up causing trouble, or even splits, perhaps over issues that have nothing to do with their real concerns. The process may take years, but if capable people are alienated from the leaders in their own minds—as a result of insensitive treatment, or of being marginalized by leadership because of their differing theology, or because their gifts do not fit for some reason into the leadership's plans—then the real concerns and energies of such people will certainly emerge in unhelpful forms. At worst, they will effectively be forced to leave the church, or end up backsliding completely. A close friend of mine once left a church because he calculated that, in the long term, he would only end up making trouble, and he could see several other people who needed to do the same, and for the same reason.

I am not simply arguing that 'we need to find something for "our" people to do'; the energies and giftings of Christians will either be suffocated, *or* they will find an outlet, and it is rather too much for leaders to assume the ability to determine, on the one hand, whether those giftings will be allowed to function or not and, on the other hand, to decide exactly how they will be used. Those who do not fit the leaders' plans will either be smothered into silence, and probable spiritual lethargy, or they will find some other outlet for their energies, usually by creating trouble, which may give the leaders all sorts of opportunities to condemn such people for their wickedness, but will do little to advance the kingdom of God. The only other option is that they will leave the church. That may appear an attractive possibility if all leaders want is a docile fan club, but again it does little to advance the kingdom or to equip the saints.

When ministries are used in the church, they help to build up the whole body, not least the parts that do the work. More than one preacher has remarked that the very act of preaching strengthens his own faith. Those who are involved in serving and caring for others (say, the sick) find their Christian commitment extended and deepened. My wife looks back upon a time of heavy involvement in a counselling ministry, established by a friend and herself, as a period of particularly strong spiritual growth. The sixteenth-century Anabaptist Hans Denck wrote that 'No one can know Christ truly unless they follow him in life, and no one can truly follow unless they first have known him.' In our own century, the martyr Dietrich Bonhoeffer said something very similar: 'Only he who believes is obedient, and only he

who is obedient believes.'[1] The point in each case is that
doing and believing are a seamless web, in which each
reinforces the other. The distinction between them is
unreal. This is why James challenged his readers to
'Show me your faith without deeds, and I will show you
my faith by what I do' (Jas.2.18). Faith must find an
outlet in action and service or it will lose its edge. 'If the
salt loses its saltiness, how can it be made salty again? It
is no longer good for anything' (Matt.5.13). Salt retains
its saltiness by being used; it loses its flavour and ability
to affect anything by being kept too long in storage.

We should not be surprised. We learn by doing. By
looking, the eye benefits the whole body, but it also
becomes a more discerning eye. By use, muscles become
stronger, quite apart from getting things done for the
body as a whole. Of course, if this is the motivation for
an individual wishing to be involved in ministry, then
their desire is merely self-serving and not Jesus-serving.
Nevertheless, Christian leaders are bound to bear this
consideration in mind if they wish to cultivate a truly
healthy body of believers. If a side-effect of Fred's
serving his brothers and sisters is to build up Fred, that
is, in a sense, none of his business. But if I am responsible for Fred's spiritual welfare, then it is my business.

One fairly common image of the sort of person who
goes to Bible college is that of the misfit who failed to
get on with their church leaders, and thinks that gaining
a qualification will be a short-cut to being given the kind
of responsibilities that will never come their way on the
basis of their actual record in a church amongst people
who know them. There are certainly people who fit this
stereotype but, in my experience, for every one who
does there are many, many more who have a real
spiritual anointing and an immense amount to give. In
fact, very many really creative, gifted Christians find

---

[1] Cited by W. Fahrer, 'Inviting Others to Know and Follow Jesus' in
Anabaptism Today, 9.9–10; D. Bonhoeffer, *The Cost of Discipleship* (SCM,
London, 1959), p.54.

their way to theological college. However, when the subject of able people being 'squeezed out' of their churches was raised in a lecture on one occasion, one student chipped in with 'Let's face it: that's why we're all here!' There was a moment's silence, and then her remark was greeted with the approving laughter of recognition by her fellows. If the 'misfit' aspect of the stereotype does not apply in the vast majority of cases, the 'if-you-want-to-get-ahead, get-out' aspect does not seem to be so wide of the mark. As it happens, this class included many of the most talented, spiritual people I have ever met. Is it possible that our churches, far from utilizing the ministries of the saints, end up suppressing them so that existing leaders can keep their positions and force through their programmes?

Up to now, I have sought to make only those points which seem to flow more or less directly from Scripture, and to relate these to experiences, either my own or those of people known to me, and which would seem to be commonplace amongst Christians, upon which those Scriptures have a bearing. But here I would like to make a suggestion for which I am unable to cite any biblical text, although one which seems to me a logical consequence of all that we have been saying, as well as indicating a way out of a very common pastoral problem. Christian leaders frequently draw up plans and programmes for their flocks which, whilst they may be admirable, seem to bear little direct relationship to the giftings and ministries on offer amongst the people whom they lead. For example, the leadership may conclude that 'the Lord is laying on our heart to open a youth work for the young people of this town'. It may be that there are some people to hand who could be used in such a venture, but not enough. And so those who have little aptitude for doing this type of thing are, subtly or not-so-subtly, pressed into service. Miss Squibbs, meanwhile, is sixty and has had nothing to do with youth work since she attended Band of Hope as a thirteen-year old. Obviously unsuited to buttonholing drug-takers in leather jackets, it is hard to imagine someone as intelligent, active and able to witness as she is filling an out-of-sight support role. Instead, she has a desire to start a new initiative based upon giving practical help to local people in their seventies and eighties, with a view to opening doorways to evangelism. She is told that her idea, whilst good, does not square with the direction favoured by the elders at this time. Typically, she will either give up, or go ahead on her own initiative and be viewed with a certain disapproval as running a project which does not have the 'official support' of the church.

This kind of thing happens constantly. Leaders announce 'the direction the Lord is leading us', and end up alienating a number of their most able people. A more variegated and fragmented approach, but one which utilizes the real gifts and ministries actually available in the group, would have a bigger impact, even though it may well lack one central thrust or 'big idea', because it would have the backing and support of everyone, and would honour the variety of gifts, burdens, and even theological emphases, that are present. It really would be allowing 'what every joint supplies' to be used in such a way that 'the whole body' is 'joined and knit together' (Eph.4.16 NRSV). If we are equipping and facilitating 'God's people for works of service, so that the body of Christ may be built up', rather than attempting to build it ourselves using God's people as implements, then we will be anxious to see people identify, and be encouraged and released into the ministries that *they* have. We will be anxious to see them acting upon the burdens that God has laid upon *their* hearts, even if—or precisely because—they are not our ministries, or our burdens. We will be happy, in fact, to frame a programme around the gifts and ministries that are present, rather than attempt to shoehorn the people we have into our 'big idea'.

All of this may sound rather anarchic (goodness! if you've read this far, what else were you expecting?) But if it really is true that, when Christ 'ascended on high he made captivity itself a captive' and so 'gave gifts to his people' (Eph.4.8 NRSV), then it is quite understandable that the job of leaders is simply to 'equip the saints' (v.12), and then to stand aside and let it all happen. Alternatively, we could smother sensitive souls into silence, and use our energies in constant fire-fighting when trouble is caused by the more tough-minded, until they eventually comply or leave. After all, that's mostly what happens right now. But somehow, it doesn't really seem to be building up the body of Jesus.

My greatest fear, in writing this chapter and the last one, is that some readers will take hold of the points made and use them as a club with which to beat their own leaders over the head. 'You see! That's how things ought to be run around here!' Perhaps they will hiss their discoveries to their friends in corners, in an effort to increase their disaffection. Some of the moaners and groaners will discern, or claim to discern, yet more causes for complaint concerning whichever Christian group they continue to bless with their presence. It will be easy enough. After all, many of the problems described here are typical rather than unusual. To use the material here as weapons in the trench warfare of church politics, however, will be to have missed the point. It will be to play the power game. But it is precisely that power game which Jesus calls us to give up. These things are not written to be used as weapons in the very war to which they cry 'Halt!' Rather, it is that *we* might act differently, that *we* might abandon the desire to control the lambs we are supposed to be feeding, or to cultivate dependence in the saints we should be equipping and immaturity in the brothers and sisters we should be seeking to present mature in Christ. If we are not yet leaders of any kind, it is *we* who must resolve to model a different pattern if and when God should bring such an opportunity our way.

The last part of the verse at the head of this chapter should remind us forcibly of this point. Yes, every person is to be involved and included in the ministry of the church. Yes, each part must be enabled to work effectively. But what is the purpose of all these contributions? Each one 'causes growth of the body for the edifying of itself in love' (Eph.4.16). Every gift, every ministry (including the 'corrective'—if that is what it is—offered in these pages) is merely a so-called 'ministry' and a so-called 'gift' if it does not serve these ends. It does not matter whether the ministry could be described as 'leadership' or not; the same criterion applies. After listing various contributions that can be made in worship meetings, Paul makes the same point to the Corinthians: 'All of these must be done for the strengthening of the church' (1 Cor.14.26). If that is not their purpose, if the 'ministry' in question is actually serving the agenda of the person ministering rather than building up the body, then it is not 'ministry' at all. In Ephesians, he adds the not insignificant consideration that the building process takes place 'in love'. Looked at in this light, in the light of love, there is simply no place for pointing the finger at others. Rather, the finger points back at ourselves.

The inclusion of all Christians in 'ministry'—serving one another and those outside of the church—is used, Paul claims, to build up the body of Christ. Indeed, it actually fosters unity amongst believers; for the 'works of service' are to continue until 'we all reach unity in the faith and the knowledge of the Son of God'. This idea stands on its head the working assumption of most churches and Christian organizations, which is that the sheep are to be penned up neatly and led from the front, and that unity is best attained by ensuring that only the voices of the few are ever heard. According to Ephesians, it is the multiple input which, far from undermining unity, actually brings it about. This is because community, like Christian discipleship, is learned by doing. The point was well understood by the evangelical Anabaptists of the sixteenth century, who held that biblical doctrine was to be worked out, quite literally, in practice. To produce doctrine within the confines only of an academic context was, in a sense, to stand *over* the Word, rather than *under* it. Teaching was produced in the context of *being* the community of faith together. Church history shows that, as Bonhoeffer said, 'A perception [i.e. a Christian doctrine or spiritual insight, whether true or false] cannot be separated from the existence in which it is gained.'[2] We learn by doing. Together. And when we learn this way, unity is fostered.

If I might anticipate a possible criticism here, I should hasten to add that this insight is itself far from being the product of abstract study. Bonhoeffer had lived in a community of ordinands preparing to serve Christ in the teeth of the Nazi régime, and who were together working through the implications of that novel and ghastly reality. My own experience of being part of a growing community of faith in South Wales has also been, in many ways, determinative for my direction as a Christian. In that fellowship, a wide range of people were constantly active in ministries of all kinds, and amidst the diversity we prayed, worked and, yes, often argued through what it meant to be church together. But the sense of belonging thus created was immensely strong. God has since called my family and myself to different spheres of service, but we will always know where we belong. The unity has been forged, not by each assenting to an identical set of practical preferences and theological propositions, but by the shared experience of a diverse range of people making Jesus known and creatively expressing his life.

If at this point we were to leave off discussion of this sentence in Ephesians, I would feel almost that I had been guilty of some exegetical sleight-of-hand. It is not that there is no real connection, in Paul's intention, between 'that which every joint supplies' (Eph.4.16 AV)

---

[2] E. Bethge, *Bonhoeffer: an Illustrated Biography* (Fount, London, 1979), p.99.

PART IV

Hastening the Coming

TEN

Hastening the Coming

> ... to prepare God's people for works of service, so that the body of Christ may be built up until we all reach unity in the faith and in the knowledge of the Son of God and become mature, attaining to the whole measure of the fulness of Christ (Eph.4.12–13).

It would be easier to say that these verses are too hard to understand than it is to confront their full implications. 'Unity in the faith' and the kind of maturity that amounts to the 'whole measure of the fulness of Christ' seem to be so far away from our own present experience that the easiest thing to do is to consign them to heaven. Some day, we tell ourselves, these things will happen. But not in this life. Yet this is something which Paul's words here resolutely refuse to allow us to do. They appear to teach that the purpose of building up the body of Christ is 'eschatological' i.e. that it relates to the Second Coming. It is a process which will continue 'until' certain goals are attained. Before Jesus returns, he will have a mature church upon the earth, which is unified by love and 'held together by every supporting ligament' (v.16).

Indeed, it seems that it is only such a church that Jesus is coming back for. John the apostle heard a roar of voices in heaven crying that, at the wedding of the Lamb, 'his bride has made herself ready' (Rev.19.7). Jesus did not make her ready; the bride—which all Christians understand as being the church—prepared herself. Even if Jesus is active in that process (and of course, he is), it is through the activity of the Holy Spirit working in his people on earth, not by simply rapturing them out of their present, sinful, woebegone position, but by working in them until *they* get to that state of readiness. Will we dare to see Jesus' calling upon our lives, and our own ministries, in that eternal perspective?

Paul teaches the same thing: unity in the faith and in the knowledge of the Son of God is 'reached'; the whole measure of the fulness of Christ is 'attained'. The emphasis is upon what happens from below, not upon some instantaneous transformation from above. There will be an instantaneous transformation, of course, but that comes *after* the bride has 'made herself ready', not before. Seen in this light, the Second Coming is not a fixed date in God's calendar for which we have nothing to do but wait; there is something for us to do. That is why so many Christians are involved in missions, especially those which entail reaching unevangelized people groups, and providing them with the Scriptures in their own languages. They are aware that, when Jesus returns, it will be possible to say that 'You purchased for God with your blood people from every tribe and tongue and people and nation' (Rev.5.9). What these Christians are doing, as are all Christians who are building up the body of Christ and working towards the 'until' mentioned by Paul, is what Peter describes in his letter: we 'look forward to the day of God and speed its coming' (2 Pet.3.12). Again, no fixed calendars; the day depends on the saints becoming co-workers with God and with one another.

It is really hard to overstate the importance of serving

Jesus in the church and the world when our ministry is looked at in this way. The smallest service of my brother, the tiniest thing done for Jesus, is not only pleasing to him, but actually draws the day of his coming closer. Our ministry—when it *is* ministry and not self-promotion—takes on a cosmic or, as the theologians would say, an eschatological significance.

When Jesus called Peter, as he calls us, to 'feed my lambs', he was calling him, not only to personal discipleship, nor merely to a lifetime's work of serving others, nor yet simply to build up the church, but to be a co-worker in the vast purposes of God. For Jesus, and for his brothers and sisters, Peter was to lay down his life on a daily basis . . . and then to lay it down 'in one lump', as it were, by following all the way to his own cross. But each aspect, whether as disciple, servant, church-builder, or as martyr and hastener of the return of Jesus, had for him this kind of eternal importance, as it does for us. We need to stand back from the smallness of that part of the work that we are involved in, in order to see the whole. It is like the mediæval bishop who asked a group of workmen what they were doing. The first replied that he was making a doorway. The second said he was working on a tower. But the third stood back from his work, looked up at the whole structure and said, 'I'm building a cathedral.' If we will look from Jesus' perspective, we can see the whole.

Let us make no mistake. Following Jesus as his disciple is worth doing for its own sake; serving others can be very hard, but frequently brings its own rewards; and knowing that we are 'helping to build up the body of Christ' is a thrill. But knowing that all of this is going on 'until' the body of Christ comes together and Jesus returns, and that our participation hastens that day, helps us to see the big picture. It transforms our prayer-times spent alone, or our changing of the bedsheets for a sick person, or our anonymous gift to someone in need, into reassurances that we are indeed co-workers together with Jesus.

It is tempting to look at John.17.21—'that all of them may be one ... so that the world may believe'—in the same light; here Jesus also speaks about the saints being 'one' in connection with a great ingathering of new believers from 'the world'. Perhaps this verse refers to end-time developments too? We could then even construct, in wooden, literalistic fashion, a sort of causal chain of connections: every-member ministry fosters unity; unity causes the world to believe and facilitates evangelism; evangelism of every tribe and tongue and nation completes the Great Commission; this completion brings in the Second Coming. But this way of forcing disconnected verses together, however impressive it might look in a sermon, is quite unnecessary. The fact is that all of these processes are interlinked and are meant to proceed together; all of them 'hasten the coming of the day of God'. The main point is that we see the work Jesus gives each of us to do in the light of his return.

Brothers, Sisters, Friends

What might this 'mature, united church' look like? To be honest, I have little idea, as it is too far beyond my—our—experience to do more than speculate. In any case, there is no need to speculate here, for this is a book about discipleship and ministry, not about eschatology. All that concerns us is to know what we must do in the vast purposes of God. We can at least see that we are called to bring forth 'that which every joint supplies', 'works of service'. In a word, we are called to serve one another and so build up the body of Jesus on the earth.

This, of course, puts the spotlight on our relationships with one another. As children of the one Father, we stand to one another as brothers and sisters. This is a powerful idea, for it speaks of the indissoluble bond between us, one that should call forth our love and commitment. Sadly, 'brother' and 'sister' terminology for many of us has become a cliché, a form of words expressing conventional piety that is to be understood theologically rather than practically. In the late twentieth-century West, brothers and sisters are usually not even very close once they have reached adulthood and left the parents' nest for another part of the country (or for another country altogether). So the simile (which is what the biblical expression is) is not always as helpful in expressing the true nature of the case as perhaps it should be. Like some other New Testament parallels—'slaves' and 'shepherds'—some of their original force is lost in the modern context. I myself see my brother and sister rather seldom, perhaps a few times each year. Of course, we are committed to one another, would help one another in a crisis, and would stay in touch wherever we moved to, and no doubt all kinds of spiritual analogies about God's intended relationship between Christians could be drawn from these facts. But the truth is that I don't share my life in any very intimate way with my brother and sister, and haven't done since I left home at the age of eighteen. Most of us, I suspect, are the same.

Perhaps a more helpful picture for us is simply 'friends'. Can we be, will we dare to become, actual friends of the Christians around us, rather than simply calling them 'brother' or 'sister' whilst having no more than a nodding acquaintance on Sundays? Will we allow ourselves to know and to be known? If we are leaders, will we be models for those we lead by being real friends to them, or by being—and not just in a theological sense—their brother or sister? A group of Christians known to me once went through a period in which they faced, for various reasons, a range of serious difficulties; they needed both help and encouragement over an extended period. Someone emerged to provide it and, at the end of it all, one of the group summed this up in a very striking way: 'She's been like ten friends to us.' In truth she had. In Christ, she is their sister, but the love was experienced as being like that of 'ten friends'.

Perhaps we are not leaders. Perhaps our own leaders are not all they might be in this area. If so, what will we do—undermine them, or offer a different model? Will we be like ten friends—or even one—to them, and to others around us?

Eberhard Bethge expresses the nature of friendship rather beautifully. Family relationship, he says, has an existence quite apart from whether or not the people concerned are actually involved with one another's lives; 'its formal recognition sustains it'. By contrast, 'friendship is completely determined by its content and only in this way does it have its existence.'[1] If the brother-sister terminology better expresses the unconditional nature of our bond with one another, the fact is that, without 'content', this soon becomes empty words; we need to start being real friends. 'Love each other as I have loved you', says Jesus, and then, 'Greater love has no-one than this, that one lay down his life for his friends' (Jn.15.12–13). Will we lay down our lives for one another? For then we are friends indeed.

John had hung around on the edges of the conversation between Jesus and Peter by the lakeside. He had many years of life to reflect on what he had heard. Despite Peter's anxious inquiries of 'Lord, what about him?' (Jn.21.21), by the time John took up his pen in old age he knew that Peter had suffered a martyr's death for Jesus and the fellowship of the church, whilst he himself remained alive. In exhorting Jesus' followers everywhere to love and serve one another, Peter's imitation of Jesus in his death cannot have been far from his mind when he wrote, 'This is how we know what love is: Jesus Christ laid down his life for us. And we ought to lay down our lives for our brothers' (1 Jn.3.16).

Perhaps some of this has been speculative. Certainly our crying need is not for the addition of some new theory, but for a vastly heightened sense of the eternal

---

[1] E. Bethge, *Friendship and Resistance* (WCC/Eerdmans, Grand Rapids, 1995), p.91.

significance of our own actions as Christians in serving one another. As we see the urgency of Jesus' call upon our lives, the infinite preciousness of each person that Jesus has committed to our care, the need to be seeking to present one another 'mature in Christ', the imminence of the consummation of all things and our own role in 'hastening the day', then we will be the more willing to heed Jesus' instruction to Peter in that last conversation by the Sea of Tiberias: 'That—any and every other consideration—is nothing to you: you follow me. And feed my lambs.'